NEVER WASTE TIME ON THE WRONG MAN AGAIN

A 5-STEP STRATEGIC PLAN TO STOP WASTING TIME AND FINALLY FIND "THE ONE"

MICHELLE JACOBY

Difference Press

Washington, D.C., USA

Cover design by: Jennifer Stimson

Editing: Cory Hott

"Full of smart, easy-to-implement strategies and fun, relatable stories, Michelle Jacoby shows women a clear and easy path to lasting love. What a great read!"

— RACHEL GREENWALD, *NEW YORK TIMES* BESTSELLING AUTHOR OF *FIND A HUSBAND AFTER 35: USING WHAT I LEARNED AT HARVARD BUSINESS SCHOOL* AND *HAVE HIM AT HELLO*

"*Never Waste Time on the Wrong Man Again* is a must-read for any woman who is thinking about giving up on love or has put herself out there again and again with no success. Jacoby helps women understand why they end up in the wrong relationships and presents a roadmap to finding an amazing life partner. She teaches women how to cultivate the right mindset, develop a dating plan, set strong boundaries, and date strategically by sharing entertaining stories of her clients and herself with honesty and humor."

— TERRI ORBUCH, PHD, PSYCHOLOGIST, RELATIONSHIP COACH, AND AUTHOR OF *FINDING LOVE AGAIN: 6 SIMPLE STEPS TO A NEW AND HAPPY RELATIONSHIP*

"Brilliant! This is one book that I will be buying by the dozen for my clients! There are so many self-help books that explain the 'why' (i.e. why do we continually date the wrong people). The 'why' is interesting but leaves us with the ultimate question, 'What do I actually do?' Michelle answers this question with specific tools that are easily accessible in a concise and detailed manner. Michelle's delivery is not only empathetic but strategic and precise."

— MARJORIE KREPPEL, LCPC, NCC, MA, DBT-LINEHAN BOARD OF CERTIFICATION, CERTIFIED CLINICIAN™

"I wanted to get married and have a family, but at thirty-eight, I was still single and felt so discouraged. Within several months of learning Michelle's techniques and implementing her five-step plan, I met my husband, and now we have a daughter. If I had continued to date on my own, I would probably still be single. *Never Waste Time on the Wrong Man Again* is going to change so many lives!"

— ELIZABETH C., COACHING CLIENT

"I've spent years with men who were the wrong fit and have spent lots of time recovering from heartbreak. Michelle's approach gave me exactly what I needed to find the right person to share my life with. Michelle's insights and her compassionate approach are a gift to her clients and readers."

— STEPHANIE D., COACHING CLIENT

"If you follow the strategies outlined in this easy-to-follow, comprehensive book, you will easily eliminate unhealthy men and find your partner. The most amazing man is out there waiting for you. *Never Waste Time on the Wrong Man Again* will help you find him!"

— BONNIE G., COACHING CLIENT

CONTENTS

To my husband, Rob, who loves me the way I've always dreamed of being loved.
Thank you for sharing this wonderful journey with me.
I love you.
And to my amazing clients who have entrusted me with their hearts. Working with you has truly been an honor, and watching you fall in love has been one of the greatest pleasures of my life.

DATING SUCKS

E ven though it's never been easier to meet single men than it is right now, finding the right man to date has never been harder. There are literally hundreds of online dating sites and dating apps that should make it easy to find love, but they don't. If you've tried online dating, I bet you're feeling disappointed and frustrated. Wouldn't it be great if you could simply swipe right on a handsome guy, send a few text messages, meet him for a drink, have instant chemistry, fall in love, and live happily ever after? Fat chance! Even though we have these amazing online platforms where you have access to literally thousands of single men, finding the right guy is actually quite hard. Does this ring true for you?

At a dating conference I attended a couple of years ago, an executive of one of the largest dating sites in the world explained that the average user on a dating site spends eleven hours online in order to go on just one date. Who the hell has eleven hours to spend on a computer, especially after spending an entire day at work? That's exhausting. And it's also an inefficient use of your time. Did you know that one-third of online daters never actually go on a date? That means one-third of all men you could potentially talk to online will completely waste your time. If the men you've dated have flaked out on you, you deserve better.

What makes online dating even more frustrating is that a lot of men lie. I'm willing to bet you've met men who exaggerated their height, lied about their age, or posted ancient photos. And while I'm bitching about online dating, let me also point out that people can be downright rude. Some disappear or send annoying texts like "Hey, what's up?" but they never actually ask you out. Or worse, they cancel at the last minute or don't show up at all. It's incredibly thoughtless.

I'm not saying online dating sites can't work. They can. Nearly half of all relationships start online. But the majority of my clients who've tried online dating say it's frustrating. For them, an overflowing inbox feels totally overwhelming. And keeping up with their emails feels like a second job. If you relate to that feeling of overwhelm, you know how stressful and exhausting online dating can be.

I work with some pretty high-profile clients who hire me as their matchmaker specifically because they don't want to put themselves "out there" and date online where their colleagues or clients can see them. If you don't want to date online, that's okay, but meeting men is going to be even harder. Since you probably shouldn't date someone from your office, you'll have to brave crowded happy hours and singles events, flirt with strangers and ask your friends to set you up. Meeting someone worth getting to know can be hard, but it is definitely doable, and later in this book, I'm going to teach you some helpful strategies that will make meeting quality men so much easier.

Eventually, you will meet someone who seems great, but when you meet him, how will you know if he's the right guy? It takes time to discover who you're really dating. During the first three months or so, you'll be dating his "representative," not the real him – not yet.

Will he be ready for a commitment? Will he be emotionally healthy? Will he have his life together? Will he be someone you can trust? Or will he have lots of issues you'll have to deal with down the road?

In my twelve years working as a matchmaker and dating and relationship coach, I've found that one of the most common reasons women remain single is because they invest their time and energy in the wrong men. The majority of my clients come to me after a failed relationship that lasted months or even years. Deep down, they knew things weren't right, but they stayed in the relationship, giving it their best because most women are loyal, goal-oriented optimists who don't want to give up, especially when they love someone. Does that sound like you? If you're like most women, you've also invested your time (and heart) in the wrong man (or men). How much time did you waste? How much heartache have you endured? Making an effort and putting yourself out there again and again without success can feel demoralizing. And spending time in the wrong relationship can mess with your emotional well-being.

I know what it's like to feel lonely and miss having a

partner in crime, someone to plan fun adventures with instead of going by yourself or deciding which girlfriend to invite. When I got divorced in my mid-thirties, most of my friends were married. Even though some of them included me when they went out, I often felt like a third wheel. Even worse, some friends had dinner parties or planned get-togethers and only invited couples. I'd hear about the fun I'd missed after the fact and feel sad that I hadn't been invited.

Holidays can be particularly difficult. Going to a company holiday party alone, heading home solo to visit family and having no one to kiss at midnight on New Year's Eve – all of those scenarios can put a damper on what should be a special time of year.

Maybe you're a single parent like I was, and you're dealing with all the pressures of parenting alone. I remember sitting at the dinner table with my kids feeling like someone was missing. It took a long time for that feeling to go away.

I do have good news. By the time you finish this book, you'll have a new perspective on dating and a new, highly strategic plan for attracting, investing in, and choosing the right man as your partner. You'll learn how to attract the kind of quality men you'll be excited to meet, you'll understand how those men think and act, and you'll date strategically. You'll learn how to easily spot red flags, you'll spot them early on, and you'll know exactly how to deal with them. Instead of feeling frustrated and hopeless, you'll feel empowered and full of hope. I promise, if you implement the strategies in this book and follow my advice, you will never waste time on the wrong man again. If you trust the process I teach you and change the way you date, you will attract the ideal partner into your life. I'm excited for you.

Before I can teach you those strategies, you need to understand why you believe dating is difficult. Is it because:

- There are more single women than men, and the playing field isn't even?
- Some men are shallow and only want to date beautiful younger women with perfect bodies?
- You live in a town or a city where there aren't a lot of quality single men, and you think a different location might work better?
- You've met players who just want to have sex and aren't interested in commitment?
- There are a lot of socially awkward men who you have no interest in dating?
- A lot of men are broke or don't have their lives together?
- You always seem to attract narcissists?
- A lot of men lie and resort to gaslighting or cheating?
- The men you like don't want to date you?
- It's hard to reject people because you don't want to hurt their feelings?

If you identify with any of the bullet points above, you're not alone. I've heard all of these reasons (and more) before. No matter what you believe is holding you back, this book will show you how to be successful and find "the one."

If you're like most women, you've put yourself out

there over and over again. I read recently that the average person falls in love four times in her lifetime. That means you've probably had a broken heart about three times before. If that's the case, I'm so sorry you've gone through that kind of pain. I know from experience how much a broken heart hurts. I've had mine broken several times (I'll tell you my story later). If you've been in a relationship that didn't work out, or one that was difficult and you spent months or even years loving someone you're no longer with, you're definitely not alone.

Many of the women I work with hire me after being in difficult or unhappy relationships. Some need therapy and time to heal in order to move on. Many wasted time on men who were:

- Negative
- Critical
- Abusive
- Cold
- Avoidant (sabotaged intimacy)
- Controlling
- Passive-aggressive
- Manipulative
- Emotionally unstable
- Emotionally unavailable
- Unkind
- Insecure
- Jealous
- Irresponsible
- Narcissistic

And who:

- Had low self-esteem
- Wouldn't commit
- Lied and gaslighted
- Cheated
- Couldn't get their lives together

If any of that sounds familiar, you probably know what it feels like to be anxious and to walk on eggshells or to question your gut or even your sanity. Being in a drama-filled relationship is exhausting and deeply sad. If you've spent time in a relationship like that, I'm so sorry you went through such a tough time. It's difficult and confusing when you love someone, but they make you unhappy. It takes a lot of courage to walk away from the wrong relationship. For some people, it takes many years.

If you've wasted time in the wrong relationship, I don't ever want that to happen to you again. That's why I wrote this book – to give you strategies and tools that will ensure you never waste time in a toxic relationship or invest in the wrong man again.

I bet you're not used to failing. You've had so many wins in other aspects of your life, like your hard-fought, satisfying career and your amazing friendships, that it's especially upsetting when you can't accomplish the one thing you want most – to find "the one." If you feel embarrassed because you've failed, please know it's okay. The people who love you understand and will support you no matter what. Sometimes you have to fail in order to learn the most important lessons in life. Everything you've been through has made you the person you are today. And the lessons you've learned from the past will serve you in the future; I promise they will.

When life hasn't turned out the way you planned, and the partner you've dreamed of is nowhere to be found, it's hard to feel optimistic. It may be hard to believe, but I assure you, now is the time to feel hopeful because everything is about to change. Your heart is resilient, and you are not broken. If you don't feel lovable, I assure you that you are. If you're not over your ex, you will let him go. If you're angry as hell, the anger will fade. If you're afraid you can't trust again, I assure you, you can. If you're afraid to give because your ex took so much, you will enjoy giving again. You will. And if you're scared that you'll always be alone because nothing has worked, please don't worry. Your beloved is out there, and you will meet him when the time is right.

If you don't feel hopeful right now, I get it. Many of my clients felt frustrated and hopeless when they were dating too. Some even felt discouraged up until the day they met their future husbands. Even I felt hopeless at times. But now, I'm happily married to a wonderful man. (I'll share more about him later.) Sometimes it's difficult to remain optimistic. This book is going to teach you the skills and strategies you need to feel hopeful and stay the course.

So, if you're contemplating giving up on love and being content with the way things are right now, please don't. Yes, you have been blessed with friendship, family, a satisfying career and more, but that doesn't mean you can't have it all. You deserve to have an amazing partner who adores you. You're a good person. You have a huge heart. You're caring, generous, and deeply kind. Of course, the Universe has good things in store for you.

If you're meant to have an amazing partner, why has he been so hard to find? Because you needed to learn certain lessons and have certain experiences so you can recognize him when he shows up. The lessons you've learned will help you choose him. Sometimes we can't see the bigger plan, so we need to have faith, stop worrying and simply trust the journey. You need to meet the present moment with acceptance and with gratitude knowing that he's on his way.

When you're done reading this book, you'll know exactly how to find your partner. You'll know how to recognize the right man instead of getting stuck in the wrong relationship. And once you find "the one," you'll finally be able to plan those vacations, create the home you want, and build a family; maybe you'll even get that vacation home you've always dreamed about. You'll be able to wake up next to your partner on Sunday mornings and say, "What do you feel like doing today?" And if you're lucky, you'll have the pleasure of growing old together.

What will it mean to you to finally find him? Imagine how happy you're going to feel. All the pressure of dating will be gone. Lonely weekends? Over and out. You'll have someone to have fun with every day. Someone who's always got your back. Someone you can look up to and respect. Someone to get naked with whenever you feel like it. That part will be delicious.

Do you know what's crazy? He's out there right now watching Netflix or walking his dog; he's doing some-thing right this second. And when you meet him, he'll be ready for you because he's already learned his lessons and had the experiences that will help him recognize you when the time is right. You just need to find each other. I'm going to show you how.

The word my clients use to describe how they feel when they meet "the one" isn't "chemistry." Instead, they almost always use the word "comfortable." And when you finally meet your future partner, you'll feel comfortable too. You'll feel like you've come home to him.

You're going to love the way he makes you feel. You'll feel relaxed. You'll be your best self when you're with him. Your friends and your family will tell you how happy they are for you and how perfect you two are together. No matter what you've been through in the past, you'll be able to trust him completely. And he will love you the way you deserve to be loved. He's going to love you right.

In this book, I'll teach you my simple five-step strategy to find your amazing life partner. With a clear plan and strong boundaries in place, you'll be able to let down your guard and date with an open-heart, unafraid of being hurt. Imagine that! You'll be able to lean into dating knowing no one can hurt you or waste your time ever again. Girlfriend, I so have your back.

One of the smartest and quickest ways to meet your future husband is to stop wasting time dating the wrong men. It's easy to get stuck in the wrong relationship, and it takes courage to move on, to face the unknown, and to believe there's something better out there for you. But there is. Using the same tools and strategies that have worked for me and for hundreds of my clients, I'll show you how to stop wasting time on the wrong men, so you're available when the right one shows up. Once you've learned the strategies in this book, it'll be easy to tell who's wasting your time. I'll show you a quick and easy way to break up with the wrong guy so you can create space in your life for your future husband. And once you've found him, you'll start the next chapter of your beautiful life together.

2

BELIEVE IN LOVE

I f you were to meet me now, you'd see I'm a successful matchmaker and love coach with a thriving business who's left a trail of happy couples behind me. And I have the most wonderful husband and family who I adore. My public persona as a matchmaker and coach shows the perfect picture. Not only have I matched and coached hundreds of singles who've found love over the years, I've also shared photos and talked a lot about my amazing husband, Rob, on social media and in my posts, not only because I want singles to know there are great guys out there (there most certainly are), but because it's great advertising. After all, if I have a handsome, adoring, kick-ass husband, so can they.

We're a good team. We have four kids, we're a playful family, we love to travel together and have a lot of fun. It's true that he's my best friend, and I often talk about our relationship when I'm coaching clients because it's a healthy and happy relationship, the kind my clients aspire to have. But what most people don't know when they look at photos of my husband and me is that it took a lot of time and personal work to get to where I am now.

When I began my matchmaking business back in 2009, I was single. I didn't meet Rob until later, and finding him was a long and often difficult journey. When I look back at the long road I traveled to end up in this marriage, there are a lot of painful memories. I've learned a lot of lessons along the path to a happy and healthy marriage. It took a long time to find a man who loves me this way.

I met my first husband right out of college, and we got married when I was twenty-three. When I was thirty-five, he abruptly left me for one of my friends. Our kids were six, eight and nine years old when we separated. I'll never forget the day we sat our kids down to explain that our family would never be the same again. That was the hardest thing I've ever had to do.

The months that followed were incredibly tough for me and for my children. But life goes on, and I'm a strong person. Within months, I decided I wanted to meet someone new. Looking back on my early forays into dating though, I cringe when I think about how bad I was at it. I made so many mistakes. In the decade between my divorce and marrying my current husband, Rob, I dated a lot and was in several "interesting" relationships.

The first man I dated after my divorce picked me up for our dates in a limousine and took me downtown to shows and fancy restaurants. That was lovely, but after a while, something seemed off, and I eventually learned he couldn't afford a car and lived in his parents' basement (he was in his mid-forties). All the glitz and glamour was just for show, and he was lying about himself the whole time.

Next, I fell hard for a handsome doctor. We dated for a year, fell deeply in love and talked about building a life together. But then one day, out of the blue, he dumped me without an explanation. Did I mention he had a problem with prescription drugs and alcohol and was in a heated custody battle with his ex-wife at the time? Oops, silly me.

Later that summer, I went into a grocery store to get some food for a barbeque and came out with a phone number. I had met the man I would date for the next four years. We had crazy chemistry and a lot of passion and decided to move in together with our kids. It felt good to feel like a family again. He loved my kids, and I loved his. We laughed a lot. He was a jokester, and it was fun sometimes.

But it was also bad. For four years, I endured jealousy, criticism, gaslighting, manipulation, passive-aggressive behavior, and I walked on eggshells. We fought constantly. My pillowcase was covered with mascara stains that would not come out. Our love for each other and our strong physical connection kept us together way too long. I think my biggest regret is that I allowed him to alienate me from my friends and family.

His manipulation was so flawless, like a frog in boiling water, I didn't even realize it was happening. Over the course of our relationship, we broke up five or six times (I lost track), but we always got back together, until the time he left our relationship for good. He married an attractive younger woman four months after we broke up. You do the math.

After our relationship ended, I spent a lot of time trying to process what had happened. Having been gaslighted and manipulated so deftly was a lot to come to terms with. For months, I found myself Googling him late at night, longing for him and hating him at the same time. Honestly, I was a little pathetic.

Even though I was heartbroken, I didn't give up. I kept on dating and finally met a handsome guy I liked on Match.com. He was into me which felt good. But a couple weeks after we met, he confided he was wearing an ankle bracelet provided by the police department. He told me a long story about his ex-wife lying to the police and – I kid you not – I believed him and kept dating him. He seemed so sincere. I remember a hot day in August when we were hanging out with friends by the pool, and the ankle device he wore under his jeans started beeping incessantly. Talk about awkward. Needless to say, that relationship didn't last long or end well.

So, there I was, after a bunch of failed relationships and months spent dating online (I even went to speed dating and singles events and got set up by friends), I had picked another guy with major issues who lied and brought drama into my life. I thought, What the fuck am I doing? I decided to take a break from dating. I was distraught.

One morning, a month or so after I broke things off with ankle bracelet guy, I drove my kids to school then came home and got in the shower. I stood under the hot stream of water for almost an hour and cried until the water ran cold. Then, I got out of the shower and stared at myself in the full-length mirror. I looked thin, drawn, and tired. Mostly, I just looked sad.

I sat on the green carpet in my bedroom wrapped in a tan bath sheet looking in the mirror at myself and said out loud, "You're almost forty years old. How can you be so fucking smart and still keep picking the wrong men over and over again?" Then silently, I asked myself, "Why can't I get it right?" I got into bed with wet hair and spent the rest of the afternoon under the covers crying until it was time to pick my kids up from school. I had no more tears left by then. I'd run out.

Later that night, when my kids were asleep and the house was quiet, I lay in bed and prayed. And then, I made a decision that would change my life forever. I promised myself I would never waste time on the wrong man again. Never again would I allow a man to tear me down, make me feel like shit, lie to me, deceive me, manipulate me or treat me poorly in any way. I promised myself. I made a vow. And I swore to God that this would be a turning point for me.

The next day, I sat down at my desk with a notepad and started writing. I wrote for hours, digging deep and looking honestly at the mistakes I'd made over the years. I thought about the choices I'd made, the relationships I'd been in, and the patterns I had repeated. When I was done writing, I had come up with a clear and precise dating plan for myself that I was determined to implement. The plan consisted of strict rules, strategies, and clear boundaries I laid out for myself. I vowed to follow the plan no matter what. I even swore to God that I would follow it to the letter.

As soon as I started dating with my new plan in place, I knew I was onto something. All of a sudden, I started meeting a much higher caliber of commitment-minded, emotionally healthy men than I'd ever met before. Over the next year, I had several drama-free relationships with nice guys who just didn't end up being "the one." Then finally, on an evening I'll never forget, I met my wonderful husband, Rob, at a restaurant bar. Our first date lasted eleven hours. (We made out and watched HGTV until 6:00 a.m.) The rest is history.

The five-step dating plan I created the day after my long cry in the shower changed the course of my life. It gave me the confidence and tools I needed to attract healthy men and make better choices for myself. The plan's strong boundaries and easy-to-follow rules kept me from dating the wrong men like I always had. Instead, I finally found "the one," and I've never been happier.

It occurred to me then, that if my plan could help me find such an amazing man after my long and difficult road, it could probably help my clients too. I began teaching my new strategies to my clients like Nicole and Chelsea.

MY CLIENT, NICOLE

My client, Nicole, was a successful businesswoman in her early forties who had never been married. After two decades of consistent dating that resulted in several disappointing long-term relationships, she decided to hire me as her dating coach. On our first call, Nicole, feeling frustrated and hopeless, cried for half the session saying things like, "I'm going to be alone forever," and, "Relationships never work out for me." It's my job to hold space for my clients, and I understood how Nicole felt. Everything she had tried and every relationship she had ever been in had ended in heartbreak or disappointment. I did my best to comfort her. Then, I assured her that doing things differently would get her different results, and I asked her to trust me and my process. She agreed to do everything I told her to do, and we began working together. Over the next few weeks, I taught her all of the lessons and strategies in this book.

With newfound confidence and a new set of tools in her dating toolbox, Nicole was then able to make much better decisions. She could easily identify men who were a poor fit, and then move on quickly. She could also tell which men were marriage-minded and genuinely interested in her. Although it was still hard at times, Nicole persevered, and I'm happy to report she is now engaged to an exceptional man who absolutely adores her. I look forward to attending her upcoming wedding.

MY CLIENT, CHELSEA

After a difficult twenty-six-year marriage to an extreme narcissist, Chelsea left her marriage with little self-confidence. Since she had married her high school sweetheart right out of college, she had no dating experience and hired me to teach her how to date. One of the things I loved about Chelsea was that she took notes during our coaching sessions. I joked with her saying she must have been a straight A student (she was). Chelsea took everything I taught her seriously and followed my rules to a tee. As our coaching sessions came to a close, and after meeting several men who were not a fit, she finally met a gentleman named Chris who, as far as I could tell, was a great guy. Two months later, I received a note from Chelsea that said, "Chris is a really good man that I probably would have dismissed if I hadn't been one of your clients. You were so right...you shouldn't be with someone who makes you anxious and when there is something that bothers you, you should speak up. I can't thank you enough for all the confidence you instilled in me. It was there all the time... just in hibernation!" For the first time in her life, Chelsea had the tools to advocate for herself with confidence and enjoy an easy relationship with an emotionally healthy man. It was a thing of beauty to witness.

I have a folder in my email where I've saved dozens of emails like Chelsea's. Helping frustrated women find their loving partners is my calling and has been the most wonderful privilege and honor. Over the past decade, the five-step plan I created for myself has helped hundreds of my clients to date in a different way in order to find healthy, lasting, drama-free relationships. These strategies work for all women, not just the ones who've been in toxic relationships. Even my widowed clients in their sixties and seventies and my younger, inexperienced clients in their twenties, have had great success. No matter who I shared these dating strategies with, the outcomes were always the same. Once they learned and utilized my five-step strategy, they were able to avoid wasting time on the wrong men and find healthy relationships much more quickly. The same thing is going to happen to you.

Now that I'm ten years into a happy marriage, when I look back at the men who hurt me in the past, I'm grateful I knew them. The lessons I learned from those failed relationships helped me find my wonderful husband and helped me teach my clients how to find love as well. So, I'm grateful. I've found that gratitude feels a lot better than anger and regret. I share this with my clients in hopes that they too will forgive and move forward without regret. It's true, the time you lost in the wrong relationships is time you'll never get back. But you can learn from your experiences and also from the lessons in this book, and that knowledge will lead you to your beloved. He's out there, and you're definitely going to meet him. Now it's time to get excited and to learn my five strategic steps.

3

HOW TO USE THIS BOOK

I wrote this book to help you understand why you end up in the wrong relationships and why you haven't been able to find your partner. When you understand what your blind spots are, you'll do things differently and get completely different results. As you read this book, you'll recognize what small changes you can make to bring about big changes. I'll share stories about my search for love and also about my clients, which will give you a new perspective and a new way to think about dating. I hope you find them entertaining and enlightening. I've changed the names of my clients for their privacy.

MASTER YOUR MINDSET

The truth is, if you don't have the correct mindset, you're destined to fail. But when you do have the right mindset, it will be the foundation of your success. I'll teach you how to approach dating with positivity and a playful sense of fun. I'll show you how to create space in your heart, in your mind, and in your life for your new partner, so when he shows up, you'll recognize him, and he'll be drawn to you.

If you feel stuck in any way – if you're still thinking about a past relationship, if you're angry at an ex, upset with yourself or feeling a ton of regret – it's going to be difficult for you to move forward in a positive way, and you certainly will not attract the right person. It's important to examine the past and to extract the lessons you need, and then leave the rest behind so you can move forward. I'll show you how your past experiences are the key that will unlock the door to your desired future. With a new appreciation for your past, you'll move forward with a sense of peace and confidence.

It's important to embrace, love, and appreciate yourself, and to understand your value in order to attract the kind of partner you want. You need to come to the table whole, instead of looking for someone to complete you. I'll demonstrate why valuing yourself and putting yourself first is imperative to your success, and I'll also explain why cleaning house and getting your life in order will help you avoid the wrong relationship and ultimately attract "the one."

This book will reframe the way you think about relationships and dating. Your mindset and approach to dating must shift in order to get the results you want. Mindset is the foundation of everything, and it's where success begins. I'll reprogram your thinking so you can approach dating in a way that will eliminate roadblocks and make finding your partner easier and more straightforward than it's ever been before.

YOUR DATING PLAN

Just like profitable businesses have well thought out business plans, we're going to develop a dating plan for you. Together, we'll get clear on what your goals are, and then you'll set your intentions. Doing this will set you up for success.

If you're like the majority of women I've worked with, you've probably spent a lot of time thinking about what kind of partner you want. Maybe you've even written down a long list of attributes your ideal partner will have as well as your list of dealbreakers. It makes a lot of sense to write these down, but what if you've written down the wrong things? Did you know that having the wrong list can keep you single? In Chapter 4, if you don't already have a list, I'll show you how to write one. And if you do have a list, we'll examine it together to make sure it isn't leading you in the wrong direction. Together, we'll choose the correct preferences and dealbreakers that describe your ideal partner and use them as a roadmap that leads you right to him.

In order to make sure you don't waste time in the wrong relationships in the future, you must define your boundaries. But knowing what your boundaries are is not enough. You need to know how to enforce them. I'll teach you an easy way to spot red flags and how to address them immediately. In Chapter 5, as you learn how to create and hold strong boundaries, I'll give you the exact words to use as you advocate for yourself. You'll also learn how to determine whether you should stay and work on a relationship or if it's a waste of time and you should move on. When you have and hold strong boundaries, no one can ever hurt you again. Because you know this, you'll date fearlessly and with an open heart.

With all of the dating sites and apps out there, it's relatively easy to find someone to date. But finding the right kind of man to date is the challenge. The truth is, there are a lot of nice guys out there. In this book, you'll learn the difference between a good guy and the right guy. I'll show you how to tell if someone is husband material or if he's wasting your time.

In order to date strategically, you have to understand what motivates men and how they think and date. As a matchmaker who's worked with marriage-minded men for more than a decade, I've heard them describe what they want, and I've listened to their feedback after more than two thousand dates. I have a unique, behind-the-scenes perspective of how men approach dating. I'll share that knowledge with you and teach you to use it to your advantage. Understanding how men think will make dating so much simpler and more relaxing for you. And ultimately, it will get you exactly what you want.

TRUSTING THE PROCESS

I understand how difficult it can be to do things in a new way. If you've done things one way for a long time, sticking to a new plan can be hard. That's why I'm going to give you easy-to-follow instructions that are rule-based. There will be a clearly defined right way and wrong way to do things. My instructions will be clear, and the strategies I teach will be easy to implement. In order to get the results you want, you'll need to do things differently. The best things in life happen outside of your comfort zone. If you trust me and trust this process, take a leap of faith and stick to the plan, I promise you'll see amazing results just like my client Jamie did.

After divorcing her abusive husband at thirty-two-years old, Jamie dated a long succession of men that amounted to absolutely nothing. She hired me because she wanted to get married and have a family and didn't know how to find the right kind of man on her own. Jamie grew up in a dysfunctional home and didn't have a relationship role model – all the more reason to work with a dating and relationship coach. When we started working together, even though she had invested a lot of money to work with me, she completely ignored my advice and dated a man who did not seem like a good guy. On a hunch, based on her answers to my questions during one of our coaching sessions, I decided to run a background check on him and found out he had two arrests for assault and also a restraining order. I also suspected he was married. After breaking up with him and taking a long look in the mirror, Jamie finally took my advice and started to trust the process. As soon as she did, Jamie's luck began to change, and in just a couple of months, she met her husband-to-be, a solid guy who shared her Christian values and her desire for children.

A year later, as I watched her enter the church in her beautiful flowing wedding dress with a huge smile on her face, I cried and used up an entire box of tissues. I had to reapply my mascara before the reception. That night, I had so much fun. Jamie and her husband asked me to give a speech in front of 250 people. Using my five-step strategic plan, Jamie was able to quickly interrupt her pattern of choosing unhealthy relationships and then find her husband.

She was able to do things in a new way, and even though it was hard, it was well worth it.

But what if you don't even know where to look to find your husband? You can't find him if you don't know where to look, right? Don't worry; I'll show you exactly where to find quality, marriage-minded men and teach you how to meet them. Then, once you've found a man you're interested in, you'll definitely want to "wow" him. I'll teach you some simple strategies that will make you more noticeable and irresistible to the kind of men you want to meet.

Putting yourself out there takes strength and courage. As much as you'd love to control the outcome, you simply cannot, and that can make dating stressful. Meeting strangers can be uncomfortable. But meeting a man you're excited about, now that can be especially nerve-racking. It's common for women to feel especially anxious in the early stages of a new relationship. All of the mixed feelings and emotions that come with dating are perfectly normal, however, they can be overwhelming. I'll show you a way to date confidently that is relaxing and stress-free, even fun.

Rejection and disappointment are inevitable parts of dating, and whether you're on the receiving end or the one dishing it out, it's never easy. Telling someone you're not interested is tough. That's why so many singles "ghost" one another instead of saying how they honestly feel. In case you don't know what "ghosting" means, it means disappearing when you've lost interest. You stop responding to text messages or don't return calls when you don't want to see someone again. It feels terrible to be left with no explanation or the closure you need to move on. If someone has rejected or disappointed you, it can put a huge dent in your self-confidence and your will to keep dating. And if, sometime down the road, you need to let someone know he's not a fit for you, I'll tell you exactly what to say to reject him kindly. When you're kind to others, it makes dating much more comfortable because your behavior aligns with your values. When you're consistently kind, it makes dating easier, and you're more likely to make enjoyable and more authentic connections along the way. Plus, being kind when you date gives you good karma. I'll teach you how to approach dating in a way that's not only strategic and effective, but also beautifully kind. And I'll show you why rejection can be received as a gift. Once you understand this, rejection will no longer sting, and you'll know how to turn disappointment into an opportunity.

From time to time, I'm going to ask you to stop reading to do some written exercises. The instructions will be clear, and your homework will be relatively easy. The exercises you'll do will align with what you're learning and will give you the tools you need to succeed. I've never been one to give busy work. These easy exercises will be relevant, helpful and worth it.

I'm also going to share a meditation with you that you can use along your dating journey. As you learn to set your intentions and cultivate the right mindset, this meditation will support your growth and success. My hope is that you'll use it when you're dating as well as in other aspects of your life. Connecting with yourself and with source, getting grounded, centered and intimate with your intentions is the most beautiful and effective way to approach dating and your search for love.

One of my favorite things about meeting my coaching clients for the first time is the remarkable change I see in their attitudes once they've learned some of the strategies I teach. They often come into my office feeling frustrated and negative about dating, and by the time they leave my office, just two hours later, they've got big smiles on their faces, and they're excited to try a whole new approach. Just like the clients I work with in my coaching program, by the end of this book, you're going to feel hopeful and excited to date, and you'll have an entirely new approach to dating – one that works. You will know, without a doubt, exactly what you have to do to find your partner. And you'll have the tools you need to never waste time on the wrong man again. This book will empower you, just like the lessons inside of it have empowered hundreds of my clients. Like them, if you learn the lessons I teach, do the exercises I provide, follow my instructions to a tee and make a consistent effort and don't give up, you will find "the one." And probably much sooner than you think.

4

STEP 1 – PLAN YOUR APPROACH

When you're searching for your partner, the first step in your strategic plan should be to cultivate the correct mindset. Your mindset is the foundation for everything. If you don't have the right mindset, you simply cannot be successful. In this chapter, I'm going to share some of my favorite stories to help you fine-tune yours because sometimes the smallest shift in perspective can make all the difference. Then, once I've given you new ways of looking at things, we'll develop your plan.

DATING GOGGLES

I remember the day my mindset shifted. I had a huge "ah-ha" moment I'll never forget. I was standing on the corner across the street from my bank on a beautiful Sunday morning. At the corner, waiting for the signal to change, was a dad with a toddler on his shoulders. While they waited for the light to change, the dad spun in circles, and the toddler laughed gleefully. As I watched the two of them spin and laugh, I thought, What an amazing guy. His wife is probably sleeping in, or maybe she's at yoga. Look at what a wonderful husband this guy is. Every woman needs a man like this.

Then, a thought occurred to me. What if I was in a restaurant, and the guy across the street was my blind date. What would I think of him then? This time, when I looked at him, I noticed he was short, kind of skinny, average looking, a bit nerdy and not all that well-dressed. Honestly, if he was my blind date, I wouldn't be that interested.

What?

Just two minutes before, he'd been the man every woman needed, and now, he was just an average looking schlub, someone I wouldn't want to date.

Have you heard the term beer goggles? You know, the more beer you drink, the more attractive people become? Well, I've coined the term "dating goggles." When you're looking at people from a dating perspective, they suddenly look worse, just like the dad on the corner.

YOUR DNA

I believe our tendency to be super judgmental and negative when we're dating is programmed into our DNA. Identifying what's wrong is a survival skill and how we continue to stay safe and procreate as a species. Our DNA, and this process of elimination, has helped humans survive and pick viable mates for thousands of years. In modern times, this subconscious tendency translates into all of us going on more first dates than ever but hardly any second dates at all. We're so busy judging each other, we aren't making real connections. We're hardly getting to know each other.

We're not in the Ice Age anymore. We need to tap into our higher selves to override this instinct to judge and look for what's wrong because it doesn't serve us. To find love, you'll need to remove your dating goggles, and intentionally look for what's *right*. There's something beautiful and unique in each man you're going to meet, even if he's not your future husband. When you look for the good, dating becomes much more authentic, connected, and fun. But if you judge men too soon, dating is just disappointing. Plus, you're likely to miss out on a wonderful guy.

Sometimes good guys suck at dating. Some are shy or nervous. Some talk too much and some don't talk enough. Some wear wrinkled shirts or forget to open doors or walk you to your car. Some post stupid bathroom selfies or shirtless gym pics or photos of their cars. And some send annoying "what's up" texts that make us want to scream. But that doesn't mean they're not great guys. It just means they're bad at dating.

MY CLIENT STEVE

Steve was a good guy who hired me to be his matchmaker because online dating wasn't working for him. I was delighted to work with him. Steve was a catch. He was handsome, impeccably dressed, owned a consulting firm and was a devoted father to his two darling little girls.

I decided to take a look at his online profile to see why he wasn't having any success. Steve had posted a scowling car selfie that was so close up you could literally see the pores in his nose. Honestly, he looked like a scary psycho, not a suburban business owner and doting dad. I didn't know if I should laugh or cry. And his profile essay was just terrible. Instead of writing something positive and optimistic, he listed all of the qualities he didn't want in a partner, and his grammar was abysmal.

After we started working together, I asked Steve to meet me for breakfast at a local diner and to bring a blue blazer and a couple of nice button-down shirts. I brought my camera, took some new photos, and told him to switch them out with his old ones. Then I rewrote his profile essay. I corrected Steve's grammar mistakes, shared the positive qualities he was looking for in a partner and even made his profile funny. All of a sudden, he was getting lots of emails from women. Steve is the perfect example of how a good guy can be bad at dating. Some men are clueless. Sometimes guys are just guys.

I admit it. I judged and rejected a ton of guys myself. It took me years to finally take off my dating goggles and shift my perspective. They're not just guys on dating apps, they're often good men. Each guy we see online and judge so quickly is someone's son, brother, uncle, or best friend, and he's got friends and family who adore him. Keep that in mind so you don't judge too quickly and miss out on a great guy.

EVERYONE HAS A GOOEY CENTER

I believe that every single person has what I call a "gooey center" – the part of them, under the surface, that's loving and good and kind. But a lot of people have layers that cover up their gooey centers. There are many reasons for this. Maybe they've been hurt before or they're shy or just not used to opening up. If you take the extra time to build trust and peel away the layers, most people will surprise you.

Years ago, I had a meeting with a potential client named Miles. The moment he walked into my office, I was not a fan. He was way too serious, he didn't smile – he wasn't nice at all. When we sat down together in my office, it just got worse. He was super uptight. I couldn't find anything I liked about him. At that point, I had already decided I wasn't going to work with him.

But then, I remembered my belief that every person has a gooey center. I had made a commitment to always take the time to find it. Instead of shutting down and ending the meeting, I did the opposite. I leaned in and smiled more. I gave him a few compliments. I asked a lot of questions to learn more about him. Eventually, I hit the jackpot and learned that in addition to being an attorney, Miles raised chickens in his backyard.

"Wow," I said, "that's so cool!"

Then I asked him all kinds of questions about chickens. I was genuinely interested because chickens are neat. I kept asking him questions and eventually learned he played the classical violin.

"Well, that's not something I hear every day, how interesting!" I said. I asked him all about his music, where he learned, what he liked to play, etcetera. Then, Miles's demeanor changed. As he spoke about his music, his body relaxed, and his face lit up. He was passionate about playing that violin, and it showed.

My feelings about Miles changed. As we spoke, I liked

him more and more. As I listened, I continued to lean in and to smile. I told him I thought he was fascinating and unique. He couldn't help but loosen up. And then he told me the story that sealed the deal.

A few weeks earlier, Miles' French Bulldog, Bella, had been attacked by another dog in the neighborhood. Since the attack, Miles' dog was petrified to go outside or walk anywhere near their home. You're not going to believe what Miles did for Bella. Every day, he would leave work at lunchtime and drive home, put Bella in his car and then drive to a nearby neighborhood to walk her. Every day, he'd park a little closer to home until eventually Bella could walk in their neighborhood again. What kind of guy does something as sweet as that for his dog? A really good person like Miles, that's who.

I'm glad I took the time to be curious about Miles and to find his gooey center. It would have been easy to write him off, but instead I took the time to know him. Are you judging the men you meet too quickly, or are you helping them shine? What a gift it is to give a man a non-judgmental space to be authentic and share himself. I hope you'll take the time to be curious about every single person you meet. Take those dating goggles off so you can really see.

MOVING TO NEW ZEALAND

I once spoke with a woman who told me she'd moved to DC from New York because the guys in New York weren't what she was looking for, and they weren't serious about commitment. She said she gave DC a shot but that wasn't working either. She was planning a move to New Zealand because she thought men would be a better fit for her there. I kid you not. She thought leaving a country of 330 million people to move to New Zealand, with a population of five million, would open up her dating options. What New Zealand lady didn't realize is that *she* was the common denominator, not the men. Until she steps away from her scarcity story, takes off her dating goggles and takes a closer look at herself, she will never find the husband she's searching for.

I know sometimes it's hard to believe there are great guys out there, but I assure you there are. I promise good guys do exist. I know they do because I've worked full-time as a matchmaker for well over a decade, and in that time, I've met hundreds, maybe even thousands, of smart, successful, lovely commitment-minded men. If you date from a place of scarcity, you'll never be successful. You've got to date from a place of abundance instead. Your guy is definitely out there.

YOU ARE IN THE EXACT RIGHT PLACE

You've been through a lot, and you're frustrated because you've wasted so much time. You've searched for years, but no matter what you do, you haven't been able to find your partner. I know you're tired and frustrated, but what if I told you you're exactly where you are supposed to be? Has it ever occurred to you that your soulmate might not be ready to meet you yet? What if he's been in a marriage that's ending now? What if he had to grow inside of another relationship to become the partner you'll need him to be? Each experience we have teaches us what we need to learn, and everything happens when it's meant to. Your partner will show up at the exact right time.

A few years ago, Bethany hired me as her matchmaker. Her husband had died in a tragic accident several years before, and she was ready to fall in love again. Bethany's had been a happy marriage, and her loss had been profound.

When I met Bethany, a tall, stylish, movie star-esque brunette with big brown eyes and a warm personality, I liked her instantly. She told me she was ready to fall in love again. I promised her I'd do everything I could to find her match. I always work hard, but for Bethany, I worked *extra* hard. For an entire year, I searched and interviewed dozens of the most amazing men I could find. I tried and tried, but no matter what I did, I could not get Bethany into a relationship. I just couldn't find her match.

A few years after we worked together, Bethany sent me a friend request on Facebook, and I accepted. It was fun to see her posts pop up on my timeline every once in a while. Then one day, while I was scrolling through my timeline, I saw that Bethany posted wedding photos. Oh, my goodness, I thought, Bethany got married! She and her handsome groom, a tall rugged-looking blonde, made a gorgeous couple and looked so in love. I was so happy for her.

I sent Bethany a direct message on Facebook. I wrote: "Bethany, I saw your gorgeous wedding photos, and I am so incredibly happy for you! I wish you and your husband so much happiness. I only wish I could have been the one to find your husband for you. With love, Michelle."

Bethany instantly responded, "Dearest Michelle, I

adore you. I know you did your very best to find the right man for me, but that was an impossible task. Because at that time, my Troy was 2,500 miles away separating from his wife. It just wasn't our time to meet, and there was nothing you could have done to connect us. We were destined to meet exactly when we did."

Honestly, hearing that was such a relief. I had felt bad for years that I hadn't been able to find her second husband. But there it was. There was no way I could have found him. It was an impossible task. Bethany and Troy were meant to be together, and they met exactly when they were supposed to meet. She had lost so much, and now she was happy again.

After that happened, I thought about Bethany a lot. I'd spent years in the wrong relationships wishing things had been different, frustrated that I couldn't find "the one." But what if everything had happened according to a bigger plan? What if I wasn't meant to meet "the one" until I was in my forties?

My hubby is so romantic he often says he wishes we'd met twenty years earlier. But, honestly, if I'd met Rob back then, I don't think I would have appreciated him or chosen him. I still had so many lessons to learn. Regardless, there was no way I could have found him all those years ago. He was living in another state with his ex-wife. Thank goodness both of our lives finally conspired to bring us together at the exact right time. The same thing is happening in your life.

You are an amazing person. You are kind and thoughtful and caring, of course you're going to meet your partner when the time is right. If you can fully accept things as they are, knowing you're on the right

MICHELLE JACOBY

path for you, then the idea that you're going to find the right person at the right time becomes real, and dating becomes a lot less stressful. The Universe has a plan for you; you just can't see it right now. Trust the journey and know that he's coming. You'll be able to use your many years of experience to see, appreciate and choose him when he finally arrives.

THE UNIVERSE HAS A PLAN

If the Universe has a plan for you, why do you have to make an effort at all? Why can't you just send up a prayer and let God answer it? I've thought about this a lot, and here's what I believe. God is super busy. Can you imagine how many requests God gets on a daily basis? When God looks down and sees you working your ass off, reading this book, dating online, going on dates, really making an effort, who do you think God is going to help – all the women sitting around hoping and wishing they'll find love, or the person who's working hard to find her partner?

The Law of Attraction states that whatever you put your energy into will come to you. Your desires, your thoughts, and most importantly, your actions, will manifest what you desire. You know that old saying, "You create your own luck"? That's the law of attraction at work. You've got to make an effort and do your part, and when you do, the Universe will help you out. Whether or not you want to figure the Universe or God into the equation is totally up to you, but it certainly can't hurt to ask for a little help.

40

A SACRED ENDEAVOR

Your search for a partner is a sacred endeavor. You're looking for the most important thing that exists - love. That's why I want you to consider that every action you take that brings you closer to "the one" is special and sacred and should be treated as such.

When I sit down at my desk and open my laptop to log into my matchmaking database to search for matches for my clients, I often take a moment to sit quietly and ask for assistance. I know, without a doubt, there is a higher power helping me connect my clients because I get way too lucky to take all the credit. I'm definitely receiving help. And so are you.

When I was single and at my most frustrated and lonely, I never stopped believing I'd find love. I had faith that the Universe had my best interests at heart and had a plan for me. Each night when I went to sleep, I said the following prayer. "Thank you in advance for the wonderful man you're going to send my way when the time is right." I didn't say, "I want to meet him next Tuesday," or, "he has to be six feet tall." Instead, I trusted that the Universe had my back and simply said, "thank you in advance." Even when it was hard, and I felt extremely lonely, I went to bed every night trusting that I'd find my love. I hope you'll end your days this way too.

LETTING GO

Since I'd never gotten it right before, and I knew my husband was out there, I decided to stop attempting to control everything, and I leaned in with faith instead. I stopped caring so much about the things on my list that hadn't worked in the past. I decided to narrow my focus to the things that really mattered, the *deeper* things. I opened up my search to men of all races, shapes and sizes. I dated men ten years younger than me and fifteen years older, I just didn't care. I also didn't care what they did for a living. Instead, I looked for an emotionally healthy man with high self-esteem and a positive disposition who was honest and kind. I asked the Universe to send me a good man, that was it. Nothing more specific. I thought I'd better keep it simple and let the Universe do the rest. Then I relaxed, stopped worrying about the outcome, and focused instead on enjoying the present knowing I'd meet the right man when the time was right.

I thought, perhaps the Universe would surprise me, and boy was I right. I ended up marrying a man who is entirely different than I'd imagined he would be. We're different religions, we come from different socioeconomic backgrounds, we have different education levels, I had four kids, and he had no kids. I'd always dated dark men, and he was blonde with gorgeous blue eyes. He even lived an hour away from me. I thought I'd marry an entrepreneur or a businessman like my ex-husband and my father, but Rob is a talented technology geek. There was so much I didn't expect to have in a partner, and yet I got everything I've ever wanted. Rob was the most wonderful surprise. I learned that trusting means letting go. That's what I had to do to find Rob. I threw away my long list of requirements and trusted the Universe to send the right man. It totally worked. And it will work for you as well.

WALK THE WALK

The truth is, no matter how much you want to meet your partner, and even if you believe the Universe conspires to help, he's probably not going to knock on your front door (unless you have a thing for pizza guys). You've got to *go find him*, and that takes determination and hard work just like everything else worth having.

If you earned a master's degree or a doctorate, I'm willing to bet it wasn't easy. You took an entrance exam, you applied to different programs, you invested financially, you showed up for class, you participated, you took notes, you did the reading, you studied, you wrote papers, and you never gave up. And when you wanted your dream job or that raise, you showed up to work on time every single day, sometimes even when you didn't feel like it. You dealt with your annoying boss, you climbed that ladder, you made those connections, you worked your ass off because that's the way it's done.

So why on earth, when you want this so badly, would you wait around and hope your husband will suddenly drop from the sky? In the words of Barack Obama, "Nothing in life that's worth anything is easy." And in the words of Dwayne "the Rock" Johnson, "Success at anything will always come down to this: focus and effort, and we control both."

There's a great Japanese restaurant called Raku near my office, and one afternoon, when I went there for lunch, I saw someone I knew across the room. I went over to the table to say hello to my girlfriend, and she was sitting with a woman I didn't recognize. Her friend looked up at me and said, "Hey, you're that matchmaker!"

I smiled and told her, yes, that was true. Then she said, in a loud voice, "Oh my God, you have to find me a guy. I am so ready! I totally want a boyfriend! You have to find me a boyfriend!"

I'm thinking, No, I don't have to find you a boyfriend. You're not my client. But then I thought, Okay, I don't want to be rude to a friend of a friend, so I asked her, "So, how many men have you gone on dates with in the last six months?" She said, "Um, I don't know, maybe three or four." Then, I asked her, "Are you dating online?" And she responded, "Oh God no, I would never do that." I gently put my hand on her shoulder, smiled, and said in the sweetest voice I could muster, "Why should I work hard to find you a boyfriend when you're not working hard to find one for yourself?" My girlfriend chuckled. Then I said to the woman, "I'll make you a deal. If you put yourself online and go on two dates a week for six months and you don't find a boyfriend, I'll take you on as a matchmaking client for free," and I gave her my business card. Of course, I never heard from her again. She sure could talk the talk, but she wasn't willing to walk the walk. The lesson here is that it doesn't matter how badly you want something, you've got to do the work. You wouldn't just wish for that master's degree, so why would you wish for a husband without doing everything you can to find him?

A common complaint I hear from men is that women are often too busy to focus on being in a relationship. Here in DC, most single women are smart, successful, career-driven women which is ah-mazing. However, when you're ready to find love, you need to make time to meet and get to know men without distraction, and long hours and business travel can get in the way. If finding "the one" is *really* your number one priority, you've got to make space in your life so he can show up. Maybe you'll have to work a little less or take fewer business trips, so you have enough time to go on dates and spend time getting to know men in order to identify someone special. Maybe you'll have to read online profiles and send messages to men when you'd rather be watching Chuck and Joanna Gaines on *Fixer Upper*, or watching *The Crown* on Netflix. Maybe you'll have to hire a babysitter or muster the energy for a date after a long day at the office. Maybe you'll have to change your bedtime and get a little less sleep. If love is your number one priority, you need to go the extra mile – educate yourself and come up with a strategy, perhaps work with a dating coach if you need some support, get a new dating wardrobe, brave a singles event; do whatever it takes if you're determined to fall in love. It would be so freaking awesome if your future husband just dropped from the sky and landed on your couch, but we both know that's not going to happen. And since you want to meet him so badly, enough that you've taken the time to read this book, why not do everything you possibly can to walk the walk instead of just talking the talk? You can't just want this. You have to take decisive and consistent action.

I laugh when people tell me it's hard to date because they're so busy. When I was single, I had three school-aged kids and a newborn who I adopted on my own, and I also owned and ran a business. I was determined to find my husband, so I hired a babysitter to watch my kids, and I went out, sometimes after they were asleep, three or four nights a week, even when I was exhausted. I'd muster the energy, put a smile on my face, and walk into the singles event or the restaurant or bar. I gave everything I had on every single date I went on. If I could do that, you can certainly find the time to do this right.

IT'S HARD, NO MATTER WHO YOU ARE

I'm going to let you in on a little secret. Before I meet with potential clients for the first time, I Google them and look at their LinkedIn profiles to learn as much about them as I can. Many of the ladies I meet are incredibly high-profile, high-achieving, powerhouse forces of nature. I'm talking highly educated and accomplished badass movers and shakers. I work in Washington, DC, and my clients' resumes are beyond impressive. Sometimes, as I sit in my office waiting to meet them for the first time, I feel pretty intimidated. I sit there thinking to myself, Who the hell am I to be giving this person advice? But then, once we start talking, and I listen to her story, I'm reminded that it makes no difference how many degrees you have, how much money you make, or whether you run an organization that's changing the world or work on the senate floor, love is elusive for all kinds of remarkable women. Love levels the playing field.

It doesn't matter how smart or successful you are, sometimes finding love is just plain hard. Our DNA isn't programmed for us to find happiness, it's programmed to successfully procreate. It wasn't that long ago that the average human being lived only thirty or forty years, not ninety years. Finding a love match, someone you can enjoy your entire life with, is quite a new endeavor. What most people don't realize is that modern dating isn't programmed into our DNA, and it isn't intuitive. It's a skill that needs to be honed.

The reason you haven't found your partner isn't because you didn't care enough or try hard enough or because you're not smart enough. It's probably because you haven't had the right mindset, the right strategy, a well-thought-out plan, or the timing just wasn't right.

YOU ARE THE DREAM JOB

Sometimes we spend so much time thinking about what we want in a partner, we forget how much we bring to the table. When you meet a man who has potential and you're getting to know each other, you might be so focused on the things you like about him, you forget that he's extremely lucky to be dating you. What do you think would happen if you decided to look at yourself as the dream job, and the men you date as applicants who are interviewing for the prized position? Looking at things with this new perspective can be extremely helpful and stop you from investing in the wrong men.

If the man you're dating doesn't impress the hell out of you, why would you give him the coveted dream job? If he shows up late or hardly makes an effort, would you give the job to him? If he said he was going to do something but then didn't follow through, would you choose him above all the other applicants? If you found out his personal finances were a mess, would you want him working for your company? If you learned he'd lied to a past employer, no matter what excuse he gave, would he be your number one pick?

You're in the process of choosing the person who will

have the biggest impact on your life – a person who will greatly affect your happiness (or lack of it) for the rest of your life. Why the hell would you give the dream job to someone who doesn't consistently overachieve and wow you?

I want you to hold every man you date to this same high standard. Day in and day out, literally ask yourself, "If this guy was applying for the dream job, would I be impressed enough to give the job to him?" This new perspective will serve you well.

BEING SINGLE IS FUN

Do you know the difference between you and me? You can flirt and kiss anyone you want anytime you feel like it (provided he's a willing participant), and I can't. Oh, those were the days. While it did get hard at times, for the most part, I had so much fun being single. There are some fun things about being single like having the entire closet to yourself, decorating your home to your taste, having control of the clicker when it's time to choose a show, picking a restaurant, and deciding who to spend your time with, to name a few. Are you so focused on what you don't have that you aren't appreciating what you do have – the freedom to meet new people, make new friends, flirt with strangers, make out, go on adventures, and make exciting choices that will impact your life?

I promise, you'll be much more likely to meet "the one" when you've cultivated an attitude of gratitude and you're determined to have fun. When you go on each and every date, decide in advance that you're going to have a great time. Even if the man you meet isn't a ball of joy, decide to *be the fun*. Bring your brightest energy to each and every date, be positive, be silly, and be playful. If you do that, not only will being single be much more enjoyable, you'll also be pretty darn irresistible. Like attracts like, so when you raise your vibration to a higher plane, you'll definitely attract the right kind of men.

Being single isn't only about meeting men. It's a great opportunity to invest in your friendships and to grow your social circle. If you meet a nice man but he's not the one for you, consider being friends. He may turn out to be a hiking buddy. Or maybe he'll fix you up with one of his buddies. I must have twenty male friends who I met on dates when I was single. I even have some female friends I met by going on dates.

A friend fixed me up with a good-looking successful businessman named Bobby. We went out to dinner and had a nice time together, but we weren't a romantic fit, so we decided to stay in touch as friends. A full year later, Bobby went on a date with a woman named Linda. They weren't a fit, but Bobby thought Linda and I would like each other, so he asked me if he could introduce us. I said, yes, absolutely, so he gave me Linda's number, and a few days later, the two of us were enjoying sour apple martinis at a local restaurant bar.

The minute Linda and I met, we knew we'd be besties. We've been close friends ever since. It's been more than twelve years since Linda and I met, and we've traveled together and started a book club. But wait, there's more. Right after I met Linda, she invited me to a party at her house, and I met a bunch of cool people there, many of whom I'm still friends with all these years later. I've probably made ten solid friends through Linda, and she's probably met even more through me. My date with Bobby thirteen years ago was the gift that just kept on giving. I'm so glad Bobby and I decided to be friends.

You never know if someone is crossing your path for a reason, so always be kind, have fun, and be open to whatever comes. A few of the men I met when I was single joined my database, and I've matched them with my clients. One gentleman I met on a date over a decade ago even hired me as his matchmaker. When you meet someone new, you don't know what will come from it, so be open. The time you invest meeting people isn't only about finding your husband. There's so much fun to be had and satisfying connections to be made, so please keep that in mind.

When you're looking for "the one," getting frustrated is natural, and it's inevitable. Here's why. As human beings, we're designed to move toward comfort (success) and away from pain (failure). If you only make dating about meeting "the one," then every time you go out or meet someone new and don't meet your husband, it'll feel like you've failed. It's incredibly difficult to stay motivated when you fail over and over again. It's the opposite of how we're designed.

So, how can you overcome the frustration of dating and stay motivated and positive? By creating opportunities to succeed. I teach my clients to have small achievable goals every time they go to a singles event, a happy hour, a party or out on a date. Your goal could be to walk up to a stranger to say "hello," to make a friend, to look totally hot, to be really kind, to be a great listener or simply to have a wonderful meal and enjoy some good company. Don't be so focused on the outcome that you can't see the forest for the trees. Be mindful and present and allow yourself to succeed. Your positive attitude will emanate from you and attract a man with a similar vibe. You want to meet someone happy and positive, right? Create those small opportunities for success, and you'll enjoy dating a whole lot more, I promise.

Now that you've come to the end of this chapter, I hope you'll take a moment to reflect on how your perspective may have shifted and how you can do things differently moving forward. Are you clear about your priorities and ready to do whatever it takes to walk the walk instead of just talking the talk? Are you ready to have faith and let go of control knowing the Universe has a bigger plan you can't see? Are you ready to try a new way of doing things, even if it's a little bit uncomfortable? Are you able to see dating as an adventure, and can you simply enjoy the ride without worrying about the endgame? A brand-new approach will bring about a brand-new outcome. I hope you'll move forward with a sense of fun, an open heart and the clear understanding that you most certainly are the dream job, and you will definitely meet "the one."

GET GOOD WITH YOU

I would be remiss if I didn't check in to see how you're *really* doing. Before you can invite the right person into your life, you need to make sure you're happy with your life first. For two reasons: First, if you're happy, you'll attract a man who's also happy, and that's a good thing. Second, if something important is missing in your life, you'll choose or stay with the wrong man for the wrong reasons. If you're broke, you may choose a wealthy man. But being rich doesn't mean he'll treat you right. If you're estranged from your family, and you date a man who's close with his wonderful family, you may stay with him when you shouldn't because you love the way his family makes you feel. If you haven't cultivated friendships, you might choose a man with lots of friends. Having friends is great, but if he's not the right person, that's no reason to stay. And if you're depressed or feeling low, you're going to attract a man with a similar vibe. Negative energy attracts negative energy. Positive energy attracts positive energy. Always keep that in mind.

In the movie *Jerry McGuire*, I hate it when Tom Cruise looks into Rene Zellweger's eyes and says passionately, "You complete me." I hate it because it's Hollywood bullshit. No one can complete you but you. You must come to dating feeling happy and whole rather than looking for someone to make you happy and whole. When you love yourself and the life you've built, that's when you'll attract the most amazing man.

I'm not saying things have to be perfect, they rarely are. But if you want to invite the right man into your life, you've got to make sure your life is right where you want it to be. If you have some personal work to do, please set this book down, reach out to a therapist or whomever you feel will support you, and take good care of yourself. Sometimes, you have to walk through the hard stuff to get to the other side. And then, when you're ready, come on back. I'll still be here to help you find "the one," I promise I will.

5

STEP 2 – DEFINE YOUR NEEDS

What if I told you that, based on my many years of experience, you're probably looking for the wrong qualities in a partner, and it's keeping you single? You've spent a lot of time, maybe even years, thinking about what your future husband will be like, and I commend you for being so thoughtful about your search. In theory, all that careful consideration is a smart move, but in reality, well-thought-out planning can keep you from finding "the one." In this chapter, you'll learn exactly what you should be looking for, and you'll throw away all the stuff that's getting in the way of your success.

When my client Rachel came to my office for the first time, I liked her immediately. She was warm and funny, and like most of my clients, her resume was impressive. Rachel held two PhDs from Ivy League Universities, and she was a successful economist. After leaving a long and unsatisfying marriage, Rachel was excited to have her first post-divorce relationship and to fall in love.

For over a year, Rachel had spent time on sites like Match.com and eharmony with absolutely no luck. Frustrated, she reached out to me for help. In our first meeting, I asked Rachel to explain how she'd been approaching online dating. More specifically, I asked what criteria she'd been using to select men online. "I usually look for Jewish men who have high-level professional careers like doctors, CEOs and lawyers," she said. "And I never respond to anyone who doesn't have a master's degree or higher." Rachel felt she should be with someone similar to herself; a successful, Jewish, and highly educated man.

I decided to tell Rachel about my husband. "I'm Jewish, and my husband Rob is Catholic," I said. "And I have four kids, but he didn't have any. I'd always dated dads because I thought they'd "get" me and understand my priorities. The night I met Rob, I assumed he wouldn't want to date me because I had four kids (my youngest was only four), and he didn't have kids. Do you know what he said to me?" I asked. "He told me he loved kids and had always wanted them."

It turned out Rob was amazing with my children, especially my youngest who I'd adopted on my own. Years later, after Rob and I got married, he legally adopted our son, and we gave him Rob's last name. It was the happiest ending I could have ever hoped for. And I had always dated dads. Thank goodness I met Rob by chance at a restaurant because he definitely would not have shown up in my Match.com searches. I didn't get exactly what I wanted, and that turned out to be a good thing.

"I always thought I'd marry an entrepreneur," I told Rachel. "My dad ran his own business for forty years. I have my own business too. But Rob is in IT and has a job;

he doesn't have a business. He's not super wealthy, but I love that he's down-to-earth and only works a forty-hour week. We spend lots of time together as a family which is what I've always wanted."

I wanted Rachel to understand that Rob was a surprise and that sometimes the Universe surprises us in the most glorious ways. I wanted her to see that by widening her search criteria she would have a much larger dating pool and higher odds of success. I also wanted Rachel to understand that the criteria she was currently using in her searches didn't determine if a man would be a good partner. She needed to be much more open and to focus on more important things like the qualities that would make a man a great husband. I hoped I was getting through to her.

I explained that I'd wanted to meet a man who lived nearby, and Rob had lived an hour away. I'd always been attracted to dark men, and Rob was blonde with light blue eyes. I love lectures and books and intellectual conversations, so I assumed I'd marry a highly educated man. Rob has an associate degree (he's getting his bachelor's degree now, in his mid-fifties, and I'm so proud of him). Needless to say, my husband isn't the man I was looking for, I told her. Yet, he's everything I could have ever hoped for, and so much more.

"Rachel," I said, "Let the Universe surprise you. You've got to be open to the larger plan you just can't see." I asked her, "Are you religious?"

"Not really."

"Then why date only Jewish men? And you know a lot of smart and successful men don't have master's degrees. What if a guy is amazing but works in real estate or consulting or is a nurse, would that prevent him from being an exceptional partner?"

Rachel got my point and agreed to eliminate her religious, educational and career criteria and instead focus on simply finding a good man who she enjoyed spending time with. She trusted me enough to give something new a try, and to this day, she's one of my favorite coaching clients ever.

Let's fast forward to an afternoon a few months later when Rachel called me excited to share some news. She had a new boyfriend, the chemistry was "off the charts" and they had so much in common, especially their love of dance. "You're going to love this part. He's African American and Christian. He also owns his own contracting business and is one of the smartest men I've ever met, but he never finished college!" I laughed out loud. "Sometimes the Universe surprises you!" she said. I told her how delighted I was to hear her wonderful news.

Now you know it's important to keep an open mind, but how open is too open? Isn't it smart to have a carefully thought-out list of things you're looking for to make sure you meet the right person? Yes, it is. Actually, it's important to have two lists. One will be a list of your *preferences*, and the other will be a list of your *must-haves* which I refer to as your list of needs.

Preferences are qualities you'd like to have in a partner. Your list of preferences will include things like:

- Tall
- Outgoing
- Confident
- Brilliant

- Caucasian
- Close with his family
- Loves dogs
- Catholic
- Adventurous
- Athletic
- Likes to dance
- Wealthy
- Funny and more

It's certainly good to know what you like, and a long list of preferences is a good thing to have. But it's important to understand that you'll never find a partner who has it all. In fact, you'll be lucky to find someone with 70 percent of your preferences.

If you reject a man with 70 percent of your preferences because you're waiting for a man to come along who has everything on your list, do you know what's going to happen? You'll end up with a different guy who has a different 70 percent. The key to success is figuring out which 30 percent you can live without and stick with that.

Remember, preferences are things you want but don't need. A good way to determine if something is a preference is to ask yourself a question like this: "If a man is six-feet-tall, will his height impact his ability to be a good partner?" If the answer is "no," it's a preference. If the answer is "yes," it's a "must-have" that belongs on your list of needs. Suffice it to say, I've never met a woman who felt her husband was a wonderful partner because he was tall.

A list of needs is a list of things you *must have* to feel

safe, loved, valued, cherished and happy in a relationship. These are your dealbreakers, the things you will not compromise on, no matter what. If your partner doesn't have the things on this list, no matter how amazing he is – no matter how handsome, successful, funny, brilliant, or sexy, you're not going to stay with him. Even if he's a great guy, you'll end the relationship, so be extremely careful about what you put on this list.

When I sat crying in front of that mirror fifteen years ago at forty-years-old, I realized I'd never had my emotional needs fully met in a relationship. In other words, I'd never been loved right. Maybe you've never been loved right either. If that's the case, you deserve so much more. I want your next partner to meet all of your emotional needs because you absolutely deserve it. Always keep in mind that you're the dream job, and he's the applicant. You're going to use your list as a tool to help you choose your husband.

Start by writing this across the top of the page: *These are the things I MUST HAVE for someone to be my partner:*

Then number your list with no more than eight to ten items. Your list of preferences can be as long as you like, but your list of needs should be short. No matter who you are, number one on your list must read:

#1. I must be with a man who is emotionally healthy and has high self-esteem.

It's imperative to address the role self-esteem plays in romantic relationships. If there's just one thing you take away from this book, I want it to be that *high self-esteem is the foundation for every healthy relationship and the most important quality to look for in a partner.*

Please don't confuse self-esteem and confidence. A lack of confidence in certain situations is normal and something everyone experiences. Self-esteem is defined as one's overall sense of self-worth or personal value. To me, it means a feeling of self-love and acceptance and an understanding that a person is inherently valuable and worthy of love and therefore knows how to give and receive love in a healthy way.

When two high self-esteem people are not a good fit, they typically part ways without drama or fanfare. They simply aren't a match and move on. But in toxic, drama-filled relationships, there's usually one or more partner with low self-esteem. If you think back on your most challenging relationships, I'm willing to bet self-esteem played a role. Jealously, lying, controlling behavior, competitiveness, manipulation and even passive-aggressivity are behaviors that are usually rooted in low-self-esteem. If you struggle with your own self-esteem issues, it's even more important that you find a healthy partner whose life is in a good place.

I'm not saying people who struggle with low self-esteem are not worthy of love. Every single human being is worthy of love. But you're reading this book because you've suffered heartbreak and you've wasted time on the wrong men. You're here because you've been through a lot and you're looking for the fast-track to a healthy, happy, lasting relationship, right? So, if you meet someone you suspect has low self-esteem – perhaps he struggles with addiction or was a victim of abuse and hasn't done the work he needs to move past his trauma, or if he has a terrible relationship with his family, or he suffers from mental illness and hasn't gotten the help he needs – my advice is to wish him well and then move on.

How can you tell if someone has low self-esteem? Sometimes it's not that obvious. Here are some clues.

He's negative.

People who are negative and see the worst in others tend to have low self-esteem. People who are happy see life through a positive lens. Pay attention if the man you're dating consistently notices what's wrong instead of what's right. That means you've got a problem on your hands.

He's critical.

People who are critical of others tend to have low self-esteem as well. If you're dating someone who criticizes you but continues to date you, be curious about why that's the case. When someone with high self-esteem doesn't like the way you are, he'll move on. Consistent criticism in relationships is a giveaway for low self-esteem.

He makes self-deprecating comments.

If a man says something like, "I can't believe someone like you would date someone like me," he may not understand what he brings to the table and appreciate his value. If someone is self-deprecating, pay attention.

He needs to be the center of attention.

Then there's the guy who needs lots of attention. You know who I'm talking about – he sucks all the air out of the room. He's the loudest at the party. He talks more than anyone else, and he talks about himself constantly. In my experience, a man who needs to be on center stage probably needs external validation because he has low self-esteem. There are plenty of people who are dynamic and fun to be around; that's not what I'm talking about. I'm referring to the guy who needs to feel important, maybe even superior, because he needs validation. Don't date him.

He's too perfect.

Have you ever met a man who seems perfect? He has the perfect clothes, the perfect house, the perfect car, the perfect friends, the perfect job, etcetera. Watch out for the man who can't be vulnerable. He may be trying to convince the world (and himself) that he's good enough. If the guy you're dating seems perfect in every way, pay close attention.

I've saved the biggest giveaway for last.

He can't hear what you're saying.

Watch out for the man who cannot hear what you're saying. Have you ever dated someone (or even had a friend) who often took what you said the wrong way and felt insulted or hurt a lot of the time? Even if you had the best of intentions and made a harmless comment, their feelings were hurt, or they got angry and blamed you. The person who hears what he believes instead of what you're saying probably has low self-esteem. If you need to walk on eggshells, you're probably in the wrong relationship. Happy people assume the best and give you the benefit of the doubt. For example, if one of my friends said something to me that sounded insulting, my first instinct would be to think, I bet she didn't mean that. I assume the best from people, not the worst. If the person you're dating can't hear what you're saying, and you have to walk on eggshells, watch out. That's one of the clearest signs of low self-esteem there is.

How can you tell if a guy is emotionally healthy?

That's something you'll figure out over time, but here are some things to look for.

- Does he have healthy long-standing relationships?
- Does he get along with (or at least deal well with) his family?
- Does he have a career he enjoys?
- Does he have a nice tidy home?
- Is he financially stable?
- Does he get along with his ex-wife? (If applicable.)
- Is there a lot of drama in his life?

The life he's created for himself is the external evidence of his internal world. Beware of men who have dysfunction and drama in their lives. Healthy people build healthy lives. Their lives aren't full of drama, and they don't play the victim. You should be with someone who will lift you up, not someone who will pull you down.

Now that I've made it crystal clear you *must* choose an emotionally healthy man with high-self-esteem, what else should you include on your list of needs?

I suggest you take some time to think about your past relationships. Were there patterns or specific behaviors that made you feel anxious, angry, sad, unappreciated, etcetera? What frustrated you the most? Also, consider your long-term goals. What kind of life do you want to have? Is having a family important to you? Think care- fully about your must-have dealbreakers then write them down. Make sure you don't put preferences on this list. You can only add about eight items, so home in on what matters most.

I'll share my list of needs to help you come up with ideas.

When I looked back on my past relationships, I realized I repeatedly dated avoidant men who were not emotionally available. In those relationships, I'd never felt treasured, fully appreciated or like a priority. I always felt like I had to pull my partner in. I'd also been repeatedly criticized, and I never wanted to experience that again. Here is number two on my list.

#2: I must be with a man who is excited to be with me and who loves me exactly as I am. He shows me how he feels with his words and actions consistently every single day.

Now, I know that's a tall order, but it's what I deserve and exactly what I ended up with. My husband Rob has told me he's in love with me every single day for the past ten years. When I wake up in the morning with bad breath and bedhead, that man tells me I'm beautiful. He adores me, and he lets me know how he feels every single day. Do you know why I ended up with a man who does that? Because I wrote it down and refused to invest in any men who didn't value me that way. When you decide to have something, and you don't falter, that's what you'll get.

About a year before I met my husband, I dated a handsome Russian named Timur. Timur was a genuinely great guy. A total gentleman, he would text and call, pick me up, take me out, plan fun dates and treat, and afterward, he'd drive me home. We had great chemistry and enjoyed each other, so we decided to date exclusively and started spending more time together. After about two months, I felt like something was off. Even though he kept doing all the right things, I noticed he'd never told me how he felt about me. He didn't compliment me or say romantic things. He was my new boyfriend, and I honestly had no idea what he liked about me. Then, when I was leaving for a weeklong vacation, he couldn't say he'd miss me. When I told him how much I missed him, he didn't even respond. So, I decided to bring it up.

I thanked him for always making an effort and for being such a gentleman, and I told him how much I was enjoying our time together. Then, I asked him why he never shared his feelings. I said, "Timur," I know you like me because you're not dating anyone else, and you keep showing up, and you do nice things for me. Even so, I have no idea what you like about me because you've never told me. In fact, you've never said one romantic thing to me."

Timur's response was honest and also kind of funny. "That's exactly what my ex-wife used to say."

Since my list of needs clearly stated my partner had to show that he cared, not only with his actions but also with his words, I knew the current situation wasn't gonna fly. I asked him to share his feelings because it was important to me.

He wanted to make me happy, so he promised he'd be more expressive moving forward. Excited, I waited. After a couple of weeks, nothing had changed. For some reason, he just couldn't be vulnerable in that way. Even though he was a wonderful man who was thoughtful and genuinely into me, I ended our relationship. I didn't hem and haw, I just did it. He knew what I wanted him to do, but even though he wanted to change, he simply couldn't be more

express-
ive. Sometimes good guys want to change but can't. At the
end of the day, it doesn't matter *why* a man doesn't give you
what you need. All that matters is that he doesn't.

Here's my item number three.

*#3: I must be with a man who loves children, sees mine as a bonus,
not baggage, and who has the capacity to love my little boy as his
own. He's someone whose parenting I will respect and who my
children will always be safe around.*

Let me tell you about the sexy Spaniard, Andres. We
met online and had so much chemistry that we made
out next to my car for twenty minutes right after our
first date. I got butterflies whenever I saw him, and we
had a lot of fun together. He introduced me to his family,
and they were great. He treated me like a princess and
was 100 percent into me; I loved it. The problem was that
he wasn't 100 percent into my three-year-old son. When
the three of us were together, he didn't play with my son,
and he even made negative comments about him from time
to time. (I swear, he was the cutest most well-behaved
three-year-old ever.) One day, Andres and I were
walking through a parking garage on the way to meet his
family for dinner. I'm five feet two inches tall and was
carrying my son who was getting pretty heavy.
Suddenly, it occurred to me that Andres had never once
picked up or offered to carry my son. No piggyback rides
or putting him on his shoulders like other men I'd
dated. He just didn't seem all that interested in my kid.

Once I realized he wasn't connecting with my son, I
noticed other things too. He had three teenagers but lived

in a one-bedroom apartment. And I didn't love the way he related to his kids. It quickly became apparent he wasn't the kind of dad I wanted for my son, so, I ended our relationship. We had just returned from a fabulous trip to the Bahamas, and he was totally caught off guard. When I explained why I was breaking up with him, he promised he'd get to know my son better. But he'd already had plenty of time, and it was what it was. He just wasn't a kid person. Even though we had great chemistry, and he was truly wonderful to me, I had to move on. And I'm glad I did because I met my husband a few weeks later. If I'd still been dating the sexy Spaniard, I probably wouldn't have been out to dinner at the restaurant where I met Rob. I could have wasted years dating Andres, but it never would have worked out. I'm so glad I had my list of needs to help me end the wrong relationship so I could find the right one.

Here was number four on my list.

#4: I must be with a man who is a financial adult, someone who doesn't have debt (other than a mortgage and car). He lives within his means and will never jeopardize my financial security.

Notice I didn't say *I need to be with a rich man who makes $250,000 a year*. That would be a preference, not a need. However, having just gone through a divorce and having finally gotten my financial act together, I absolutely did need to be with a man who was responsible, someone I could feel safe with.

Sometimes women tell me they need to be with a man who earns a certain amount of money or who makes more than they do. This is a big red flag for me. When it happens, I investigate what that desire is *really* about. Maybe she experienced financial insecurity in the past and doesn't want to feel that way again. That makes perfect sense, but she needs a financially responsible man, not a rich one. Do you see the difference?

Women often say they need a man who's highly educated or super smart. But that's a preference, not a need. What they should look for instead is a man they love spending time with. At the end of the day, if he's a dummy, they'll be bored to tears. I think sometimes we expect too much from our partners. Your partner is not responsible for your intellectual stimulation; you can read a book, go to a lecture, listen to a podcast or take a class for that. If you want to be with a man who is stimulating to you, then write something like this: *I must be with a man I sincerely enjoy being with and talking to.* That should do the trick.

Your desire to have kids (or not to have them) is definitely a deal-breaker, and you should put that on your list as well. It's important that you invest your time dating men who enthusiastically share your long-term life goals.

The entire point of your list of needs is to make sure you end up with a man who treats you beautifully, who adores you, who makes you feel safe and secure, who loves you unconditionally and who is a good fit for you – a tall order but totally doable. Your carefully thought-out list will also ensure you don't waste time on the wrong men. But for it to work, you have to be willing to walk away from a good guy if he isn't meeting your needs. Period the end.

Remember, an amazing man does not always equal an

amazing partner for you. Ask for what you want, and if he doesn't give it to you, accept that without judgment and move on. When you meet your future partner, he'll be an excellent fit, and you'll be glad you didn't settle.

Remember, the fastest way to find the *right* partner is to stop wasting time on the wrong men. Don't invest your time in something that's destined to fail. Don't continue dating someone while wishing things were different or that he was different. Don't fall in love with potential. He is who he is. The most important thing you can do is to love yourself enough to insist on getting what you need. When you do that, you create space in your life for your life-partner to fill, and the Universe will deliver.

Now it's time to write your list of needs. Please set aside this book and get to work. I suggest you type it and then print it out and keep it in a spot where you can refer to it regularly. Each time you date a new person, refer to your list. You know what you need to do, so please write your list of needs now.

6

STEP 3 – ESTABLISH YOUR BOUNDARIES

If I had a nickel for every time a woman told me she attracts the wrong kind of men, I'd have a boatload of nickels; I'm talking a big boat, like a yacht. A woman told me recently that narcissists are drawn to her like moths to a chandelier. Gurl, please. While I did my best to be empathetic, I had to tell her the truth and explain that there is no such thing as attracting a narcissist. There is also no such thing as attracting avoidant men, needy men, emotionally defunct men, passive-aggressive men, liars, or cheats. The truth is you don't attract them; you choose them. It's as simple as that. And while that may be a little tough to hear, it's good news because making new decisions will bring you a new outcome. You are in charge of your destiny and can make better choices in the future. In this chapter, I'm going to show you how to make those better choices. I'll teach you how to create and hold strong boundaries to ensure you choose the right men and don't waste time on the wrong ones. Don't worry, once you know how, it's easy to do.

If you've dated the wrong men in the past, it's important to own the fact that you chose those men as much as they chose you. You allowed them to have access to your life, and you decided to stay in a relationship with them, even when you knew something was wrong. When I ask my clients to share the red flags they ignored in the first three months they were dating their exes, they can almost always name the behaviors they chose to overlook. The saying "hindsight is twenty-twenty" is so true. Looking back, you will probably agree that you swept red flags under the rug hoping things would get better. Why did you ignore the red flags? Perhaps you ignored them because you're an optimist and see the best in others. Maybe it's because you're loyal and believed if you hung in there, things would change. Maybe it's because you're a giver and wanted to do whatever it took to help your partner grow and be happy. Maybe you stayed in the wrong relationships because, despite the things that were wrong, there were also certain needs that were being met, and they were important to you at that time. Or maybe you simply hung in there because you'd already invested so much time, you didn't want it to be for nothing. You didn't want to give up. You wanted to see it through.

I stayed in a toxic relationship for four years because I wanted the companionship and the physical connection, the financial security was comforting, and I loved being a blended family. In addition to all of the painful parts of that relationship, there were a lot of good things too. Almost every bad relationship has aspects that are good. And most men who behave badly have qualities that are good as well. That's why we love them, because we see the part that's beautiful and focus on that part instead of what makes us sad. But where does that get us in the end?

I've wasted years in relationships that made me feel bad more often than they made me feel good. The years I invested on the wrong men are years I can't get back. Having said that though, I wouldn't change a single thing because I've been able to use the lessons I learned to build a business that helps people find love. I took the pain I experienced, and I learned how to use it to help create happiness in other people's lives. I've also had four amazing kids who I adore. And I found my amazing husband Rob. So, no, if I could go back, I wouldn't change a thing.

The day I cried in the shower and questioned myself in the mirror was a turning point for me. I remember later that night lying in bed quietly talking to God and telling Him I'd learned so much from my mistakes. I thanked God for the tough love but asked if I could please just meet my husband now. I was ready to put the past behind me and put the lessons I'd learned to the test. The next day, I created the rules and tools I'd need to ensure I stopped choosing the wrong men. And after those rules and tools worked successfully for me, I taught them to my clients. For more than a decade now, the tool I'm about to give you has helped hundreds of women stop wasting their time on the wrong men.

Before I get down to business and share this tool with you, I want to make sure you're moving forward without regrets. How can you do that? By understanding that every single person who has touched your life has had a hand in you becoming beautiful you. I'm certain I would not have appreciated or chosen my husband if I hadn't dated the men who hurt me first. Like the lyrics of my favorite song *Bless the Broken Road* by Rascal Flatts, I'm grateful for the broken road that led me straight to him.

Please don't beat yourself up for the choices you've made. You're subconsciously programmed to choose the wrong men, at least according to one of my favorite authors, Harville Hendrix, the founder of Imago therapy who wrote the international bestseller, *Getting the Love You Want*. The premise of Imago therapy and also his book is that when each of us is young and impressionable, when we're forming our understanding of love, relationships, and gender roles, the people who raised us, whether our parents, aunts, uncles or caretakers, will inevitably frustrate us in some way. Whether we had an overbearing parent or an absent parent or anything in between, the people who raised us set the stage for how we identify and experience relationships throughout our lives. If you were raised by critical parents, criticism might feel normal to you even though it's hurtful, and you might gravitate toward critical men without even realizing it. If you grew up in a family with a lot of yelling and arguing, you might feel at home in a high-drama relationship that doesn't serve you. If you had an absentee parent or a parent who pulled away when there was a conflict, that feeling of not getting enough love might lead you to choose men who are avoidant (uncomfortable with sustained intimacy) even though you want a partner who can emotionally connect. We gravitate toward what feels normal to us, even when it isn't healthy.

We're not all destined to that fate, but Dr. Hendrix's theory rang true for me and for the majority of my clients, so I want you reflect on what your "normal" might look like so you can better understand your past choices. The strategies in this book will help you avoid your "Imago Match" (the person you subconsciously choose) so you can find a healthy relationship.

When I met my husband, Rob, he was so different from the avoidant men I usually dated, that at first, being with him felt a little weird. All of the attention, his sincerity, and the deep emotion he brought to our relationship made me feel uncomfortable. He almost seemed too eager. Instead of pushing him away though, I sat with my discomfort because I knew that I deserved a man like him. It took me a while, but after some time, I was able to appreciate and enjoy everything he brought to the emotional table and into my life. As you embark on your journey to find your partner, it's helpful to reflect on your childhood family dynamic and the role models who taught you about love and relationships. Then, reflect on who you've chosen to date in the past, and see if there are any patterns. To stop wasting time on the wrong men and find the right partner, you have to decide to date differently, even if it's uncomfortable at first, because you're worth it.

Please have the deepest empathy for yourself and your experiences. Each person you've loved has touched your life for a reason. There were lessons you needed to learn along the way in order to grow and develop into the person you are today. Now that you've learned so much, it's time to use those insights to find your partner, and it's my privilege to show you how to do that. I want you to have the healthy, happy, easy relationship you deserve.

To ensure you don't waste time on the wrong men in the future, the most important thing I can do is to show you how to develop strong boundaries and then enforce them. The most important tool I created for myself and now teach to my clients to help them avoid the wrong relationships is called a protective contract. You will use your protective contract to define your boundaries, identify and address the red flags in your relationships, and assess whether you should continue to date someone. Instead of sweeping issues under the rug, you'll quickly and decisively advocate for yourself from a place of strength. This tool will show you exactly who to invest in and who needs to hit the road. When used properly, it will help you avoid spending years, maybe even decades, with the wrong person.

In order to find love, you can't be guarded. In fact, there's no way to make a deep emotional connection with a man and be guarded at the same time. Intimacy is created and grows when you are open, honest, and authentic. You must approach dating with an open heart if you want to fall in love. But what if you've been lied to or cheated on, and it's hard to trust someone new? What if you don't even trust your gut anymore? If you feel scared and vulnerable, that makes perfect sense. But don't worry. Once you have this tool in place and know how to use it, you can safely date with an open heart because no one will be able to hurt you ever again.

In the first few weeks when you date someone new, the truth is, you're dating his "representative." In the beginning, as you're getting to know each other, he'll give you his best and show you what he wants you to see. But after a while, the real person will show up with all of his human foibles and flaws (we all have them). That's when the red flags are likely to show up, so pay close attention.

Think about your past relationships and what your exes did to make you feel anxious, sad, angry, taken for granted, or unloved. In addition to romantic relationships, think about your friends and family too. Remember all of the behaviors that didn't serve you. Now, I want you to write them down.

Open up a Word document or pull out some lined paper and a pen and write down the words, "my protective contract," at the top of the page. Next, number the page and write down all of the negative behaviors you've experienced (and don't ever want to experience again). Number them, and then begin every sentence like this: "I will not date a man who…"

Your list might look like this:

1. I will not date a man who is passive-aggressive
2. I will not date a man who criticizes or insults me
3. I will not date a man who doesn't keep his word
4. I will not date a who has anger management issues
5. I will not date a man who compartmentalizes me
6. I will not date a man who has addictive behaviors

You get the idea. This list can be as long as you like, so put a lot of effort into remembering the behaviors that made you feel bad. You can also add additional negative behaviors you don't want to experience if you wish. Once you've finished your list of negative behaviors you will not accept from a partner, the next step is to bullet point specific examples underneath each one. For example.

1. I will not date a man who is passive-aggressive

- He gives me the silent treatment
- He acts sullen or angry but won't tell me why
- He purposely ignores my honey-do list
- He stays away when he's angry.
- He shows up late because he knows I hate that

2. I will not date a man who criticizes or insults me on a regular basis

- He makes negative comments about my body
- He says negative things about me in front of our friends
- He tells me I'm stupid
- He makes fun of my sense of humor (in a mean way)
- He criticizes the way I parent my kids
- He criticizes my diet

3. I will not date a man who doesn't follow through

- He says he bought me a gift, but he never gives it to me
- He says he's going to go to my work party, but he doesn't go
- He says he'll drive me somewhere, but then he changes his mind

- He says he's going to take me on a trip, but then he doesn't invite me
- He says he's going to plan a surprise for me, but he never does
- He says he's going to introduce me to his kids, but he doesn't do it
- He says he's going to fix something for me, but he doesn't
- He says he's going to call me at a certain time, but he doesn't

4. I will not date a man who has anger management issues

- He yells and screams at me when he's upset
- He honks and yells at other drivers and cuts people off
- He gets into fights at bars, especially when he's drinking
- He loses his temper with his kids and yells at them

5. I will not date a man who compartmentalizes me

- He doesn't introduce me to his kids
- He doesn't introduce me to his family
- He doesn't introduce me to all of his friends or his work colleagues
- He doesn't tell his friends about me
- I can't drop by his office to say hello
- We only stay at my house, never at his

- I don't have a key to his home even though he
has a key to mine

6. I will not date a man who has addictive
behaviors

- He has an issue with gambling
- He drinks too much and too often
- He watches porn almost every day
- He smokes weed almost every day

These are just a few examples of behaviors that you might list. The possibilities are endless.

The last thing I want you to do is to sign and date this contract. This is a contract between you and yourself, and you are committing to only date men who treat you beautifully because that's what you deserve. I suggest you print this out and keep it somewhere safe where you can read it whenever you want. You might even want to frame it. Some of my clients do.

Now that you've written down the behaviors you won't tolerate, what should you do with your list? When you're dating someone new, review it regularly. The moment you notice one of these behaviors you've written down is occurring, you must have a conversation with the man you're dating immediately. Speak with him in person – not on the phone or by text – and say something like this:

"Before we met, I decided I would never stay in a relationship with someone who criticizes me. I'm not sure if you're aware of it, but you criticize me a lot. You make comments about my

body and make mean jokes about my intelligence, and you also
correct me in front of my friends. Your critical comments don't
work for me, and they need to stop. If you continue to criticize
me, I'm not going stay in this relationship."

If he doesn't understand what you're talking about, give him specific examples.

Did you notice I used the phrase "doesn't work for me" several times? I didn't whine, complain, act needy, blame or vilify him. Instead, from a place of strength, I clearly stated that his behavior didn't work for me; that's all. His behavior might work for someone else, but it doesn't work for me. Did you also notice the definitive statement at the end, that if the behavior didn't change, the relationship would end? That's how you've got to say it, because he needs to know your terms are non-negotiable. This is a "come to Jesus" moment for him. He'll know he needs to change his behavior, or he'll lose you. First, he'll have to decide if he wants to change his behavior. Then, he'll have to decide if he's capable of changing his behavior. The two are not one and the same.

When you give him this ultimatum, there are three different ways he might respond. The first is to get defensive, argumentative or deny his behavior. He might even flip things around and blame you. Blah blah blah, who cares. If he pulls that bullshit, dump him on the spot. You took the time to address a problem in your relationship, and he wasn't able to hear you, empathize with your experience, and have a respectful conversation. Do not date him anymore – period. He's not your husband.

The second thing that can happen is that he acknowledges his behavior, he apologizes, and he promises to change. He might change his behavior for a little while, but then the behavior creeps back in – he can't sustain the change. He wants to change. He just can't. This is the guy you're most likely to waste years on. A man like this is the hardest to leave because he's probably a good guy. The reason he can't change doesn't matter. Let me repeat that – the reason he can't change does not matter. What matters is that he can't, period, the end. As hard as it's going to be, you must stop dating this man because your relationship is destined to fail. At this moment in time, he cannot be the man you need him to be. That's all you need to know. Adios.

The third kind of response is the rarest. He acknowledges his behavior, he promises to change, and then, he does. It's rare that a man will make a change like this because a lot of our behaviors are based on old habits and unresolved issues. But this guy has the capacity to reflect and assess his actions, decide to make a change and then follow through. This is the man you keep on dating. He may or may not end up being "the one," but he's definitely worth getting to know better. I tell my clients to find a guy who "grows as he goes." The best partners are the ones who try to do better and be their best selves. They always want to grow and improve. This kind of man doesn't change for you, he changes for himself and because he values you and your relationship.

I used my protective contract when I was first dating my husband, Rob. One of my ex-boyfriends sabotaged my friendships and wouldn't let me stay in touch with any of my exes. When we broke up, I swore I'd never let a man ruin my friendships again because they're too important to me. One of the things I wrote on my protective contract was: "I will not date a man who negatively impacts my friendships in any way."

A few months into my relationship with Rob, he told me he didn't want me to be friends with my ex, Eric. Two of Rob's exes had been unfaithful, so he felt uncomfortable with me being friends with an ex. My friendship with Eric was completely platonic. We didn't see each other often or talk all that much, but our friendship was important to me, nonetheless. Because this scenario was written in my protective contract, I knew I had to talk to Rob immediately. I sat him down and explained that ending my friendship with Eric didn't work for me. I was not his ex-wife or ex-girlfriend. I was trustworthy and had never given him any reason to doubt me. Then I told him he needed to get comfortable with my friendship with Eric and get to know him, or I would not continue to date him. Keep in mind at that point I suspected Rob was "the one," so I had a lot to lose. I had committed to leaving any man who separated me from my friends, so I stuck to my contract.

This issue was a trigger for Rob because of his past experiences, but he wanted to be with me, so he stepped outside of his comfort zone, and he changed. One day, I came home from my office, and Rob and Eric were shooting hoops and drinking beer in the driveway. Rob had reached out to Eric and invited him over. That meant a lot to me.

Because you've been hurt before, it might be tempting to dump someone the first time you notice a red flag. Don't do that. Instead, use your protective contract and give him the opportunity to change if he can. He might surprise you the same way Rob surprised me.

I'll tell you right now, some of the people reading this book are going to write their protective contracts and then ignore them and keep dating the wrong men. It's tough to break old habits. That little subconscious voice in your head is going to do its best to lead you astray. Please don't let that happen. Trust the process, use your protective contract and the words I've shared with you. Be strong and hold your boundaries. If you use it well, your protective contract will ensure you are never treated poorly in a relationship again.

If you had a protective contract when you were dating your ex, how long would he have lasted? When should you have walked away? I'm willing to bet, if you'd had your list of needs and protective contract in place years ago, you wouldn't have wasted all that time on the wrong men.

In my email there's a folder where I keep success stories, testimonials and thank you notes from happy clients. One of my favorite emails is from a client named Mary who was in one of my group coaching programs. About six months after we worked together, she sent a note thanking me for making her complete her protective contract. She admitted she'd been skeptical when I made the group complete them. But she'd done the exercise anyway and printed hers out. She told me she had just ended a relationship. She wrote, "If I hadn't worked with you, I probably would have dated him for four years instead of just four months. Thanks to my protective contract, I knew I had to end it and was able to break up with him without doubting myself. I appreciate you sharing this tool with me."

Here's a visual I want you to think of when you're

dating. Imagine there's a football field full of men – lots and lots of them. You're in one endzone and your future partner is somewhere down at the other end of the field. You don't know exactly where he is, but you know he's down there waiting for you. As you meet and date men while you're moving down the field, you don't want to get stuck on the ten-yard-line and leave your guy waiting. I want you to assess each man you date, and if he isn't "the one," move on down the field quickly. Swat them out of the way so you can move down the field toward your love. The fastest way to find the right man is to leave the wrong man right away. Now that you have your list of needs and your protective contract to help you move down the field, don't let the wrong man stand in your way.

7

STEP 4 – PLAY IT COOL

I was sitting on the proverbial couch in my therapist Patricia's office telling her about one of my girlfriends, Lindsay, who wasn't making an effort in our friendship. Sure, she'd answer the phone when I called, and she was happy to see me when I stopped by her house to visit, but she never called me or came to my house. She didn't even return my phone messages most of the time. We'd known each other for decades, and I considered her one of my closest friends, but I was feeling hurt by her lack of effort. She never initiated anything.

Patricia suggested I "play poker" with my friend. She explained that in the game of poker, we have two choices when it's our turn to place a bet. We can "see" the current bet, which means we meet it, or we can "raise" the bet, meaning we up the ante and increase the bet. She instructed me to "see" Lindsay's efforts but not to "raise" her. In other words, she wanted me to stop making an effort to see if Lindsay would step up. This, Patricia explained, is how to figure out if Lindsay could show up as the kind of friend I wanted her to be.

I had a talk with Lindsay. I explained that, even though we were close friends, I initiated almost all the time, and it had been that way for years. I explained that I called her most of the time, but she rarely called me or returned my calls. I told her I loved stopping by her house, but she never stopped by mine, even though I lived closer to town, and she was often nearby. I pointed out that I invited her to parties and called her to make plans, but she rarely ever did that for me. I told her it would mean a lot to me if she'd make more of an effort in our relationship. I explained that my love language was quality time.

She responded, "Michelle, everyone gives in different ways. Whenever you need me, I've been there for you, right?" Of course, she had. We'd been there for each other for years, but that wasn't my point. I wanted my friend to show me, through her actions, that she valued my friendship, and I made that clear. I didn't want to argue. I'd shared my feelings and made my ask. I decided to play poker just like my therapist suggested. I stopped calling. I stopped dropping by. And I waited.

And I waited and waited and waited.

I patiently waited to see if Lindsay would give me a call. She didn't. I waited to see if she'd stop by my house even for a quick hello. Nothing. Nada. Zero effort from her. Fast forward six months. Yes, you read that right, six freaking months, and my so-called close friend had not called me one single time. Before I started playing poker, we saw each other or talked every single week. Since playing poker, I hadn't seen her in months. Needless to say, I was extremely disappointed and had the answer I needed.

Years have gone by, and I still haven't seen my friend. About five years after our talk, she messaged me on Facebook saying we should get together for lunch. In the spirit of friendship, I agreed and sent some dates that worked for me. She never responded. We're still friends on Facebook, and I wish her the best, but I will not be seeing her again. I don't invest my time in people who don't value me. Playing poker made it clear that my friend might have enjoyed my company, but she didn't value me enough to make an effort. Game over.

The time I used to spend with Lindsay is now available to spend time with other friends, people who are excited to be with me, friends who make me feel good. Playing poker worked so well that, to this day, I still pay attention to which friends make an effort and which friends don't. There's give and take in relationships, and I understand not every friend will make the same effort as I do. Having said that though, I will only invest in friends who make me feel valued. Playing poker works.

COULD IT WORK WITH MEN?

After playing poker with my friend, it occurred to me that playing poker might work with men too. What if I'd played poker with all the men I'd dated in the past? Would things have been different? There were so many times I'd failed to let men lead, I'd asked men to spend time with me, I'd given them gifts, I'd told them how I felt before they told me. I gave and gave and gave.

I'd surprised one boyfriend, the doctor, by stocking his fridge and pantry with $500 worth of food on move-in day. I'd detailed his car with a toothbrush, removing food and gum his kids had left behind. I'm a serious giver, and I'm always looking for ways to do nice things for the people I care about. The problem, I realized, was that my exes didn't do those same thoughtful things for me. Not long after I stocked his fridge and detailed his car, that boyfriend dumped me.

After that, I met a handsome attorney named David, and things were going well. We were spending lots of time together. I'd met his kids, and he'd met mine. We were having fun, and I was excited. I decided to tell David how I felt – that I saw real potential for us. The next week, David disappeared. I wonder what would have happened if I'd played poker with him.

THE FIX UP

One of my neighbors asked if he could fix me up with a nice man he knew through business. I agreed and thanked him, and my neighbor gave him my number. He called, and we set up a date.

On a warm summer evening, Eddie pulled into my driveway in a Porsche convertible, with the top down, looking like a Jewish JFK, Jr. I watched from the window as he walked up the walk to the house. He knocked on the front door, and when I came out, I had to look up. He was six feet tall, and oh my, he was smokin' hot. He was wearing a crisp white linen button down shirt that contrasted with his dark tan and light blue eyes. And then he smiled. Oh. My. God. Those perfect white teeth. And the dimple. Did I mention he was a self-made millionaire?

We went out to dinner, and the conversation was wonderful. Not only was he handsome and successful, but he was also a genuinely nice guy, a class-A human. I was smitten. He had everything on my list. At the end of the date, we made out. It was ah-mazing.

A few days later, he called to ask me out again, and when we saw each other for the second time, we had a great time, just like we had before. We went to dinner at an outdoor cafe, we took a walk in town, and we kissed again. I was seriously into him. Over the next several weeks, Eddie kept asking me out. We saw each other about once every ten days. We always had fun. The chemistry was good. I really liked him.

THE PHONE CALL

One day, about two months after we met, Eddie called to ask me out just like he always did, but this time I didn't say yes. Instead, I thanked him for asking but explained that I didn't want to date him anymore. I'm pretty sure that sexy hunk of a man had never heard anything like that before. "What?" he said. "Why?"

I said, "I know you like being with me, and I appreciate all the times you've taken me out. It's been a lot of fun, but here's the thing. I'm the kind of woman men get excited about, and I want to be with a guy who sees me on Thursday and asks, 'What are you doing Friday, Saturday and Sunday?' because he can't wait to be with me again. You're perfectly fine seeing me about three times a month.

89

I know you like me, Eddie, but let's be honest, you're just not that into me." Even though my dates with Eddie were over a decade ago, I still smile when I think of what he said next.

He said, "Okay," That was it. He didn't protest. He didn't try to explain. He simply agreed because I was right. We ended the call, and I chuckled as I hung up. Of course, I was disappointed, but I'd been spot on. Who wants to date a guy who isn't that into you? Definitely not me.

I PLAYED POKER!

During the eight weeks Eddie and I dated, I had tickets to sporting events and the theater, and I was invited to some great parties. I would have loved nothing more than to invite him to the games and the shows and to have a hot date at the parties, but I didn't invite him. Instead, I invited girlfriends or went alone. Why? Because I was playing poker. Eddie wasn't inviting me to baseball games or shows at the Kennedy Center or to meet his friends, so why should I invite him? If I had, he would have accepted, and I would have seen him much more often, probably once or twice a week, and then I would have thought we were "dating." But because I played poker, it was clear that, while he enjoyed my company, he was not excited about me. I was a busy mother of four who was running a business while looking for love. I certainly didn't have time to waste on a man who wasn't excited. I shut that waste of time down and moved on.

WATCH WHAT THEY DO

If working with men for all these years has taught me anything, it's that men show you how they feel through their actions, not with their words. If you want to know how a man feels, watch what he does. If he consistently makes an effort to spend time with you (without having sex; more on sex in the next chapter), and he's not just texting, he probably likes you a lot.

Over the years, I've taught hundreds of my female clients to play poker, and it works every time. If a guy texts you, text him back. If he calls, call him back. If he asks you out, do your best to be available. If he introduces you to his friends, you can invite him to meet yours. If he tells you he's into you, you can do the same. If he buys you a gift, buy him one too. I can go on and on and on.

CHICAGO GUY

I often pose this scenario to my coaching clients and ask them what they'd do. Now, I'll pose it to you:

Let's pretend you've been dating for months and you're totally fed up and frustrated. Then, you finally meet someone amazing. You've seen him four times in the past two weeks, and you two have talked for hours on the phone almost every night. Things are going great. He tells you he has to go to Chicago for a week on business, but he'll call you every night to check in. How thoughtful of him. So, he flies off to Chicago, and he keeps his word and calls you ever night.

Meanwhile, a couple of your girlfriends invite you to a

winery this coming Saturday. Another friend asks you to go hiking on Sunday. And there's a guy on Bumble who wants to take you out on Saturday night. All of this sounds fun, but what you really want is to spend time with Chicago guy this weekend. You don't want to commit to anyone until you two have plans.

So, now it's Wednesday night, and you're on the phone with Chicago guy. You need to know what's up so you can plan your weekend. What do you say to him to make sure he asks you out? Do you hint that you'll be free? Do you suggest a date yourself? This is where I pause and wait for my client to answer.

My client will inevitably say, "I'd either hint that I'm free this weekend, or I'd ask him what his plans are."

"Noooo! I'm teaching you how to play poker! You're not supposed to say anything to him about the weekend!"

If a man is excited about you, he'll damn well investigate your weekend plans and lock you down. A man who's into you will make it happen. And if he doesn't ask you out, go ahead and make plans with your friends or the Bumble guy. Then, if he asks you out at the last minute, thank him. Tell him you'd much rather spend time with him, but you already made plans. Ask him to please give you more notice next time so you can spend time with him instead.

In other words, show him you have a life. If he wants to spend time with you, he needs to plan ahead or he'll miss out. When you do this, you're literally training him to ask you out in advance. He'll either do it or he won't. And you'll be able to see his level of interest based on what he does.

FEMININITY IS YOUR SUPERPOWER

In addition to revealing a man's true feelings, what else does playing poker do? It keeps you in your feminine energy, which is attractive to men, especially the kind of masculine men you want to meet. Most of my clients are successful businesswomen who are used to setting goals and then doing what it takes to accomplish them. That may work in business, but it will backfire when you're dating.

Most men, whether they realize it or not, want to earn you. Men are hunters. If you're too available or aggressive, they'll usually lose interest, just like David lost interest in me when I told him I was into him too soon. I'm not saying you can't be enthusiastic or affectionate. You should be. But you have to let men lead and meet them where they are. If a man's going to fall for you, he needs to do it in his own time. If you take the reins, he'll likely lose interest.

SHE JUST COULDN'T LISTEN

I had a client named Kate who owned her own company and was a corporate rock star. She hired me as her matchmaker because she didn't have time to look for men online or go to singles events. She wanted me to vet men who met her requirements so she could meet them right away. She was in her late thirties and wanted to start a family. She was determined to find her husband as soon as possible.

Over the course of the year I worked with Kate, I

introduced her to about a dozen men, five of whom she was excited about. They were excited about Kate too, but all five of them lost interest in her after three or four dates. Here's why.

Instead of playing poker and waiting for invitations, whenever Kate was free, she'd ask the men out. She'd invite them over to her place for dinner or send them her schedule so they could make plans. She did this over and over again and never let the guys take the lead. She took the reins every single time. Kate was an action person and was simply getting things done and moving toward her goal, just like she did at work. That strategy works in business, but not in love, not with men, especially the highly successful men Kate wanted to meet. I wonder what would have happened if she had taken my advice, played it cool, and let the men set the pace. I suspect she would have ended up with one of those guys she was so excited about. But she was used to being the boss, and despite the hefty fee she paid me, she just wouldn't take my advice. When her matchmaking contract ended, she was still single. Oh well.

FIND A GIVER BY DUMPING THE TAKERS

If you're a giver, I'm willing to bet you've dated quite a few takers in the past. The dynamic is natural at first; you give, he takes, everyone's happy. But then, after a while, when you don't get your needs met, the relationship doesn't feel so good anymore. But, when you commit to give only as much as you're receiving, a man's generosity and thoughtfulness, or lack of it, will become evident quickly. If he stops giving, and you stop too, that'll usually put the brakes on a relationship.

Playing poker is a foolproof way to make sure you don't over-give and attract a taker. Instead of giving first, wait for him to give, and then enjoy giving right back. When two givers find each other, they'll spend the rest of their lives making each other happy. And that's awesome.

All those years ago, when I was hunched over the front seat of my boyfriend's car scrubbing the interior with a toothbrush, he wasn't doing squat for me. He was happy to receive $500 worth of groceries and a detailed car, who wouldn't be? I was so busy being "into" him that I didn't pay attention to the fact that I was doing all the giving. I shouldn't have been all that surprised when he dumped me. I wish I had known about playing poker back then. He probably wouldn't have lasted long.

LET'S GO OVER IT AGAIN TO MAKE SURE YOU'VE GOT IT

So, to recap, playing poker means you're going to put the onus on men to create the momentum. It's not your job to make things happen, it's theirs. You're going to be the enthusiastic and appreciative recipient of their efforts. They're going to do the work, and you're going to enjoy their efforts and reciprocate. If a man consistently ups the ante by asking to spend time with you, if he shares his feelings with you, if he does nice things for you, that means he's into you. Only date men who show their enthusiasm. Don't focus on what men say, watch what they do. If a man is just not that into you, don't waste your time. Move on.

The guy who texts you but doesn't ask you out – gone. The guy who doesn't call for weeks and then shows up – gone. The guy who doesn't introduce you to his friends or expects you to drive to his house all the time or who never asks you out and only wants to watch Netflix and chill – gone, gone, gone. If a man doesn't make you feel special – goodbye.

Do not show up in your masculine energy and turn a good man off. Do not spend time with a man who isn't into you. And do not date a taker. You deserve to be on the receiving end for once. Playing poker will call in a generous man who is genuinely excited to be with you.

DON'T MAKE THIS MISTAKE

One word of caution though. When you play poker, make sure you match his efforts. If he gives and gives and gives, and you don't do the same, a quality man will lose interest and move on.

PLAYING GAMES?

Is playing poker playing games? The answer is no. You're simply investing in men who invest in you. You're waiting to see a man's level of interest before you go all in. I don't see anything wrong with that. Understanding how men operate and having a smart strategy when you're dating isn't playing games. It's a strategic and intelligent approach that will ensure you end up with the partner you deserve.

WHEN CAN I STOP PLAYING POKER?

So how far do you have to take this poker playing thing, and when can you stop? As soon as you know for sure that he's genuinely into you, he's made a sustained consistent effort, and he's asked you to be his girlfriend, you can ease up and eventually stop and enjoy a more natural give and take. But remember to always refer back to your protective contract and your list of needs to make sure things are progressing as they should.

NOW, LET'S REFLECT

Think back to your past relationships. What if you had played poker? How would things have been different? Do you see how implementing this strategy could have changed things for you – perhaps ended the wrong relationships sooner?

THANK YOU NOTES

For years, I've received thank you emails from former clients telling me how they played poker, and it worked. There are hundreds of women all over the world playing poker right now. They're dating givers who are into them, and they're dumping the men who are wasting their time. I hope you'll do that too. You deserve to be adored by a man who consistently considers what will make you happy and then follows through. Remember, you get what you accept. Don't accept less than you deserve. Don't be afraid to walk away from a relationship that doesn't serve you. The fastest way to find "the one" is to get rid of the wrong man quickly. When you do that, you'll send a decisive message to the Universe, and you will manifest the partner you want.

8

STEP 5 – TAKE IT SLOW

My husband may kill me for sharing this, but this is an important story, so here goes.

After one of our first dates (we got drinks and then had dinner at a restaurant near my house), I invited Rob back to my house to hang out, watch some TV and, if I'm being honest, to make out. I liked him and wanted some couch time, if you know what I mean. Well, we were making out on the couch, getting a little hot and heavy, and suddenly, I stopped. I looked up at Rob and told him there was something I wanted to say. "Sure, what is it?" he asked. He sat up and waited for me to answer. Here's what I said to him.

"I like you a lot, and this is fun, but there's something you need to know about me. Right now, I'm not just dating to have fun, I'm dating because I'm looking for someone to share my life with. I decided a while ago that I'm not going to have sex with anyone until I'm in an exclusive and committed relationship. The next time I sleep with someone, I want it to mean something special." And then I told him these three things.

1. I told him I thought he was hot and that I was attracted to him
2. I told him I was a big fan of sex and playfully said I was good at it – wink
3. And I told him I was not in a rush to be in a relationship

I said those three things because I didn't want him to feel like I was rejecting him or that I was a prude. I wanted him to know that I liked him and was looking for love, but I wasn't in a rush. I continued, "If you want to get to know me, you're going to have to respect that boundary." And then, to be even more specific, with a smile on my face, I said, "We can keep things PG-13, above the waist only, for now. I'm cool with that."

I waited to see how he'd respond. Without missing a beat, Rob smiled and said, "no problem," and then we started to kiss again. From that day on, he didn't try any hanky-panky. He was 100 percent respectful of the boundaries I set. We continued to date and didn't get physical until we became exclusive about two months later, after we had spent a significant amount of time getting to know each other. Things went smoothly for us and waiting to have sex is one of the reasons why.

If you're playing the field and want to date casually, there's nothing wrong with getting naked and having fun – you do you – seriously. But if you've decided you want to find your life partner, you've got to approach dating differently. You should wait to have sex until you're in a committed relationship (we'll be talking more about exclusivity later in the book). Until a man is officially your boyfriend, you should not be having intercourse or giving or receiving orgasms, to be more specific. I strongly recommend keeping things PG-13. There are several important reasons to wait to have sex which I will cover in this chapter.

WHY YOU SHOULD WAIT

When you're intimate with someone, your body releases all kinds of hormones, chemicals and endorphins that can affect your judgment. Having sex activates and accelerates attachment, regardless of whether or not you're emotionally intimate with someone yet. In other words, when you have sex too soon, you'll experience a premature or false sense of intimacy. Doing that will also change your expectations. You may expect a man you've slept with to treat you like he's your boyfriend even though he isn't yet (or may never be).

My client Lucy had been dating Chris for about two weeks. Against my strong advice, she slept with him one Saturday night after he came over to her place for dinner. That week, on our Tuesday afternoon coaching call, she was upset. She told me that when she woke up on Sunday morning, he was gone. He'd gotten up early, while she was still asleep, to go cycling with his Sunday morning cycling group, something he did every week. She also told me he hadn't called her since their date. She wasn't sure if she would hear from him again, and she was kicking herself. "I really like him," she said, and then she cried.

Two things happened after Lucy and Chris slept together. First, she expected him to stay with her on Sunday morning, something they hadn't discussed or planned for him to do. And second, she expected him to call her the next day. I asked her why she'd assumed he'd change his regular Sunday routine. I also asked her how often he'd called her in the prior two weeks since they'd met. He'd called her about twice a week.

When Lucy had sex with Chris, her expectations changed, and she wanted him to treat her like he was her boyfriend. But he wasn't and he didn't. Chris went about his business as usual. He went on his regular Sunday morning bike ride with his riding group – why wouldn't he? He'd never called her daily before, and he didn't now. He continued to do the things exactly the way he'd been doing them before they slept together. For him, nothing about their new relationship was all that different, other than the fact that they'd had sex.

Waiting to have sex before you're exclusive is smart. It helps you maintain realistic expectations, so you don't feel prematurely attached to a man you don't know that well and who isn't your boyfriend.

Lucy and Chris didn't end up together in the end, and Lucy promised me she'd heed my advice from then on. She regretted her decision to sleep with him but also appreciated the lesson, as painful as it was. She decided to change her strategy when it came to sex, and not long after that, she met "the one."

MEN AND WOMEN APPROACH SEX
DIFFERENTLY

In my opinion, the *most* important reason to wait is to see if a man sees you as a potential partner or if he just wants to hang out and have sex – in other words, waste your time. The majority of men operate differently than women. Typically, men date and have sex and *then* fall in love whereas women date, fall in love and *then* have sex. That's usually how it works, although everyone is different. To illustrate how men operate, here's a story about my close friend Michael. Before I tell the story, I must share that Michael's a stand-up guy. He's thoughtful and kind, a loyal friend, a wonderful father, a successful business owner – a really good guy. He's also a great catch, someone I'd fix up with a close friend.

Michael had just started dating a woman named Lauren, and I was curious and wanted to meet her. The four of us, Michael and Lauren and my husband and I made plans to meet for dinner. We had a great time, and I liked her a lot. Fast forward about a month. I bumped into Michael at a happy hour with friends. He had a big smile on his face and was in an extremely good mood, so I joked with him asking if he'd recently gotten lucky. "Did you and Lauren finally do the deed?" I asked. He smiled and told me that they had in fact had sex.

"That's awesome! I'm so glad you're into Lauren," I said. Michael looked at me, smiled and said, "Actually, I'm not that into her. I don't really think it's going anywhere." What?! I asked him why on earth he'd slept with her if he didn't see himself getting serious with her. When we'd met for dinner, it had been obvious she liked him a lot. I explained to him that she probably thought he was serious and into her because he slept with her.

And do you know what my friend Michael, that good guy, said next? He said, and I quote, "That's not my problem." I was floored. When I asked him why he had sex with her, his answer was simple. He said, "Because I'm a guy. She wanted to have sex, so I was in." That was all. He was a man. Sex was available so he went for it without considering what Lauren might think or how she might feel. That was the day I realized that even good guys sleep with women they don't intend to date seriously. Simply because they can.

Not only do men sleep with women they don't want to commit to, but some men also sleep with women they're not even attracted to. Geesh, guys and women are so different. I've talked to my husband to get his take on this, and even he has slept with women just for the fun of it. For the most part, men and women approach having sex differently. If you're serious about finding a partner and don't want to waste your time, you need to know that the man you're dating is interested in you, not just your vagina and his orgasm. This is why you must have "the sex talk" early on and keep things rated PG-13 until you're exclusive.

THE DISAPPEARING ACT

Several years ago, a woman named Sophia participated in one of my group coaching bootcamps where I teach single women how to date strategically. During our eight-week coaching program, she met a man she liked. They talked every day and were seeing each other about twice a week.

During one of our coaching calls, I explained to the ladies that they should wait until they were exclusive before having sex and explained how to have that conversation. Sophia decided to give it a try and had "the talk" with the man she'd been seeing. She explained to him that even though she found him attractive and loved being physically affectionate, she would not be having sex with him (or anyone) until she was in an exclusive and committed relationship. She also told him she was not in a rush to be in a relationship.

On our group coaching call the next week, Sophia was upset. It had been six days since she'd told the man she was dating about her boundaries around sex, and since then, he'd completely disappeared. No more texts. No daily calls. Nothing. Doubting herself, she asked me if she'd done something wrong. I cut her off. "Sophia, stop! That guy was wasting your time. The minute he found out he wasn't going to have sex with you, he disappeared. He just showed you he had no intention of getting serious with you. He just wanted to hook up."

Instead of being upset, I suggested she be grateful he'd shown her his true colors so quickly. Now, she wouldn't have to waste any time on him. Instead, she'd freed up her time and energy to look for the *right* man. By disappearing, that guy actually did Sophia a big favor. Waiting to have sex discourages two kinds of men – players and commitment-phobes. And when they disappear, it's something to celebrate because getting rid of the wrong guy is a step in the direction of your future partner.

THE SELFISH SEDUCER

My client, Marie, a cute, sassy, and particular (aka picky) attorney living in Baltimore, finally met a man she was excited about. He checked off all the boxes, and she liked him. At my urging, Marie had the sex talk with this new guy. After she explained her boundaries to him, he laid off for a while but soon started making the moves, trying to tempt her to sleep with him even though she'd been clear.

I told Marie this was a huge red flag. A man who doesn't respect your boundaries or care about making you feel comfortable is focused only on himself. By trying to have sex with her, he was being disrespectful and selfish. "Is that the kind of husband you want?" I asked. "Someone who's all about himself and doesn't consider what's important to you?" I told Marie to tell him, in no uncertain terms, that if he disrespected her again, she'd stop dating him.

But she didn't take my advice. Even though he'd ignored her boundaries, she kept on dating him. After all, it had been hard to find a man who checked off every box. When they finally broke up a few months later, a heart-broken Marie sent me a note that said, "You were right. He was a very selfish man, and I don't want a selfish husband! I'll listen to you from now on, I promise."

BE A LITTLE OLD FASHIONED

In addition to respecting your boundaries, a man who's serious about you will also make a consistent effort. As I explained before, you can tell a lot about men by looking at what they do instead of only listening to what they say.

Hanging out on the couch takes a lot less effort than planning old-fashioned dates. If a man courts you – he plans dates, picks you up and is a real gentleman – the odds are better that he's genuinely into you versus a guy who just wants to come over to your house to hang out and have sex. Having sex is easy, but taking the time to *know* someone, that's a different story. That's what it's all about.

It's so easy to meet people nowadays that the bar has become pretty low, and some men are just plain lazy. But you're worth the effort. If a man wants to be with you, he'll do the work it takes to know you. He'll take the time to have conversations that build connection and create trust. And he'll take the time and make the effort to have an emotional connection with you first. He won't mind saving the sex for later.

WAITING WORKS

A man who's genuinely interested in you will have no problem waiting. In fact, when you wait, you'll be perceived as a high-value woman who doesn't have sex with just anyone. I've talked to a lot of men about this, and they all say the same thing. If a woman jumps into bed with them too soon, they usually lose interest. If a man is genuinely interested in you, he won't mind waiting. In fact, waiting can be exciting. Take it from all the men I've asked and from me, your favorite matchmaker. Waiting is a smart move that works.

BETTER SAFE THAN SORRY

There is one physical consequence of having sex too soon that I haven't mentioned, and that's your health. Each time you have sex, you potentially expose yourself to an STD or maybe even risk a pregnancy. Instead of taking a chance with your health, please wait until you know someone well enough to have an open and honest conversation about safety and contraception. Sex is personal and consequential and something that should be carefully considered and enjoyed responsibly with someone you trust.

Let's review the reasons you should wait to have sex until you're in an exclusive relationship.

1. Chemicals are released that cause premature attachment
2. You'll have inappropriate expectations, and this causes anxiety
3. You'll find out if a man is commitment-minded and genuinely interested in you
4. You'll avoid selfish disrespectful men
5. You'll both do the important work to create an emotional bond
6. You'll be perceived as a high-value woman. If something is too easy to have, most men lose interest, so make them wait
7. You'll avoid STDs and unwanted pregnancy
8. It brings up the idea of exclusivity and a way to talk about it

Here's a reminder of the language you should use to have this conversation.

"I'm dating because I'm looking for a partner, not just to have fun. I've decided I'm not going to have sex until I'm in an exclusive and committed relationship because I want it to mean something special. I'm definitely attracted to you, and I'm sure if we do have sex at some point it'll be amazing (smile when you say this). I also want you to know I'm not in any rush to be in a relationship. If you want to get to know me, you're going to have to respect this boundary."

BUT WHAT IF YOU'RE HORNY?

But what if you're horny and just want to have sex, and you don't want to wait? If that's the case, I totally understand how you feel. Go find yourself a nice guy, someone you trust, and agree to be friends with benefits. Have all the fun you want with him until you have a boyfriend. Having casual sex is fine if you know he's not "the one," he feels the same way about you, and you're both clear about your intentions.

BECOMING "EXCLUSIVE"

What does it mean to be exclusive exactly? Does it mean you're in love? Does it mean you think this person is "the one?" Does it mean you've promised to spend your lives together?

Hell no.

Being exclusive simply means you focus on getting to

know one particular person without the distraction of other people. It doesn't mean you're in love or you've promised to date him for a certain amount of time or with a certain outcome.

People often avoid exclusivity because they aren't sure of their feelings. They avoid committing because they don't want to mislead someone, hurt their feelings or waste their time. But exclusivity is an important part of figuring out who your partner will be. You need to spend more time together and have different kinds of expectations and more personal experiences to learn who someone is on a deeper level and to see how things will work out between the two of you. The relationship will be the test. You've got to try it on for size to see if it fits.

HOW DO YOU KNOW WHEN YOU'RE EXCLUSIVE?

Don't ever assume you are exclusive with someone. The only way to know you're exclusive is to have a clear and intentional conversation with the man you're dating and to agree to date only each other. Just because someone spends a lot of time with you doesn't mean you're the only person he's dating.

My matchmaking client Annabel found that out the hard way. I introduced her to James, one of DC's most eligible bachelors, and they hit it off right away. Three months in, they were spending three or four nights a week together. They'd also been on a fabulous wine tour in Napa and to Rome and Venice, Italy. As I often do, I called Annabel to check in and asked, "Are you two dating exclusively?" "I assume we are," she said. "I mean, we spend tons of time together, and we're leaving for Paris on Thursday. I can't imagine he'd be dating anyone else." It all sounded wonderful, but I told Annabel to talk with James to make sure they were on the same page. She resisted, saying that at this point, it would be an awkward conversation. But I insisted.

It took her a whole month to get up the nerve to talk to him, and when she did, she couldn't believe his response. James was a good guy, and he was completely honest with her. He told her he had been dating (and sleeping with) other women and had no intention of dating only her. The truth is, since they'd never discussed being exclusive, he wasn't obligated to date only her. He hadn't done anything wrong. Annabel was heartbroken, and the next day, she told him she didn't want to date him anymore. It took some time for Annabel to heal, but eventually she started dating again. I'm happy to report I introduced her to the man who would become her next boyfriend. He's adorable, and he adores her.

THE MORAL OF THE STORY

A man is not your boyfriend until you have a conversation and agree to date only each other. That means you both take down your online profiles, and you tell your friends and family you're dating someone. There are no secret relationships allowed. Only date a man who is excited to tell his friends and family that he's off the market because he's dating someone special – you.

WHEN SHOULD YOU BE EXCLUSIVE?

How do you know when it's time to be exclusive with someone? A good rule of thumb is to ask yourself, "if you were to walk down the street and see him on a date, would you be upset?" If the answer is yes, it might be time to take each other off the market.

WHAT IF HE DOESN'T ASK?

But what happens if you've spent a lot of time with someone over the course of several weeks, you like him and want to be exclusive, but he hasn't brought it up even though you two had the sex conversation (or even if you haven't)?

Tell him in person, not via text or on the phone, that you're in a bit of a conundrum and need his advice. Inform him that there are several men who've asked you out (you're still dating, so that's true), and you don't know what to do. Since the two of you have been spending so much time together, saying "yes" to a date feels kind of weird, you say. Then, ask him what he suggests you do. If, after dating you for a couple of months, he says you should meet other men, then he's just not that into you or ready for love, and you need to move on.

REMEMBER, YOU'RE THE DREAM JOB

The whole point of going on dates is to find someone to focus on. If a man has been on eight or more dates with you and is still looking for someone better, why waste your time? There's always the possibility he's a slow mover or a bit shy. If that's the case, asking his opinion about your conundrum should do the trick. My bet is he'll lock you down as his girlfriend on the spot. But, if he doesn't, you'll know exactly where you stand. Don't waste your time on men who aren't excited about you. You're amazing, you're the dream job, and you deserve a man who gets that and wants you all to himself.

FEELING ANXIOUS

After the initial excitement of having a new boyfriend wears off, you may find yourself feeling anxious. Having a new partner is a big adjustment, and sometimes you can feel unsure about how to navigate your new relationship. You might even feel a little claustrophobic because you're used to being alone.

When you become exclusive with someone new, it's important to have a conversation about how you'll navigate your new relationship. What will your expectations be? How often will you see each other? Will you spend weekends together? When will you meet each other's families? Will you be his plus-one at family weddings and during the holidays? Will you make travel plans without letting each other know? Everyone has different ideas about how relationships work, so talking about your hopes and expectations early on is a smart move. The terms can always change as the relationship develops, but always maintain an open dialog.

DON'T BE AFRAID TO COMMIT

Here's one last thing to keep in mind. Don't be afraid to commit to someone you like because you're not sure if it will work out. There's no way you can know for sure unless you try. If you feel there's potential with a man who respects your boundaries, meets your needs, shares your values and your goals, and he's a great guy, please don't be afraid to give a relationship a try. Remember, you can end it any time you want. All it takes is one conversation. Knowing you can walk away should take the pressure off. You'll never find love if you don't take a chance.

WHAT IF YOU JUST KNOW?

I want to end this chapter with a story about my client, Claire. Just two weeks into our work together, right after we posted her profile on Match.com, she met a man named Tim and was smitten. Claire and Tim had instant chemistry. The connection was intense, and he asked her to be his girlfriend after just one week. They had only met in person twice and had spoken on the phone three times – that was it. On our next coaching call, Claire told me she wanted to be exclusive with Tim, even though they had only met a week before.

I told Claire a man must earn her exclusivity by making a consistent effort by investing his time to learn about who she is and what makes her tick. He has to be transparent and share openly about himself. And he needs to earn her trust and her respect over time. These are things that cannot be rushed. Then, I told her my story.

I shared that just two weeks after meeting Rob, just like Tim had asked her to be exclusive, Rob told me he didn't want to date anyone else. As sweet as that was, I told Rob I didn't know him well enough to call him my boyfriend. Then, I asked him to court me – to ask me out and spend time with me until I felt I knew him well enough to accept his invitation to be exclusive. After eight weeks, once we'd spent a lot of time together, and I felt ready, I let him know, and we took things to the next level.

I suggested Claire have a similar conversation with Tim. "You barely know him, and you just paid me a lot of money to coach you. What's the rush?" I asked. But Claire didn't care. She only wanted to date Tim. She refused to respond to any of the other messages in her Match.com inbox. I spent some time thinking, and I came up with a plan.

I said to Claire, "If you want to take yourself off the market to date this guy who you barely know, fine. But I want you to tell him you won't have sex with him until you know each other well and have spent a lot of time together. That means even though he'll be your boyfriend, you won't be sleeping together for two or three months. Got it?"

Claire brought my proposal to Tim, and he accepted her terms. After about two wonderful months spent getting to know each other, they booked a fancy hotel at a spa in the mountains to consummate their relationship. To make a long story short, they got married and lived happily ever after.

At the end of the day, you simply cannot rush true

intimacy. Not only is waiting to have sex a smart strategy, but making love is much more meaningful when you truly know and deeply care about the man you're dating. Taking the time to build a foundation based on friendship and trust before having sex is definitely the way to go. A healthy and satisfying relationship is well worth the wait.

9

FIND YOUR GUY

Now that I've given you my five-step process:

1. You have the right mindset and approach
2. You know exactly what you need
3. You have strong boundaries and know how to hold them
4. You understand men and know how to "play poker"
5. And you're clear on why it's important to wait to have sex

Now, I'm going to teach you the best ways to meet single men because without men, you can't put any of what I've taught you into action.

IT REALLY IS RAINING MEN!

Women tell me all the time how hard it is to find quality men to date. And that's true *if* you don't know where to look and how to meet them. The truth is, there are wonderful single men *everywhere*, but you've probably been so busy looking down at your phone or racing to your next appointment that you didn't even notice.

Last year, I was driving into the city, and I passed a bus stop. There were about a dozen people waiting for the bus and every single one of them was looking down at a phone. These days, we're all in our own little worlds, looking at our devices, listening on our EarPods, and rushing from place to place instead of connecting and getting to know each other. No wonder it's easy to feel lonely in the middle of a crowded city. I think it's such a shame.

TALKING TO STRANGERS

I love talking to strangers and do it all the time. I treat everyone I meet as if we're already friends. I smile, say "hi" and chat with people at the grocery store, at the bank, or even just walking down the street, and they're usually nice to me. But if they aren't nice, that's about them, and I don't sweat it one bit. I'm not going to let anyone keep me from being warm and friendly because that's my jam. I have fun with strangers every single day. My mom says I've always been like this. She says I used to make her worry because, when I was little, I'd smile and talk to strangers on the New York City subway.

You're probably thinking, well, talking to people is

easy for you because you're an extrovert. Actually, I'm not an extrovert. I think the reason I feel so comfortable chatting with strangers is simply because I do it all the time. Like anything else, practice makes perfect and over time, things get easier.

I challenge you to put down your phone and take a look around. When you do, you'll notice the smorgasbord of delicious men who cross your path every day. Unless you live in the middle of nowhere or never leave your house, you're bound to run across men worth meeting. How do I know this? Because men need to get their hair cut, buy groceries, renew their drivers' licenses and go to the gym just like you.

If you're shy or an introvert or uncomfortable talking to strangers, here's something you can try. Instead of thinking about talking to strangers as being outgoing, look at it as sharing your warmth and kindness wherever you go. I mean, who doesn't want to spread kindness and good energy, right?

Start small and chat with the people you see every day. That might be a coworker, a parking attendant or a neighbor who walks her dog when you walk yours. When you see them, smile and say "hi," and maybe even share a genuine compliment. When you do this, your only goal should be to make sure that when you walk away, he or she is smiling. That's it. Your only goal is to make them smile.

Next, start chatting with people you come into contact with like the lady who rings up your groceries at Whole Foods or the guy who holds the door for you in the lobby of your building. One day I was going to get my teeth cleaned, and as I was headed up to the fifth floor where my dentist's office was, there was an older gentleman riding the elevator with me. He must have been ninety years old, and he was dressed in a crisp blue suit. When I got to my floor, before I got out, I turned to him, smiled and said, "You look really dapper today." I could see him smiling as the doors closed. Being friendly and kind is fun.

The more you practice talking to strangers the easier it will get and the better at it you'll become. Once you've had a lot of practice and feel more comfortable, then it'll be time to start talking to men you're attracted to. That's a little tougher, but you can do it. Just practice and don't worry about the outcome. Even if you just exchange a smile or a few words in line at Starbucks, that's okay. Keep doing this, and you may be surprised at what happens. When you chat with a man, you're giving him permission to continue the conversation. And if he's interested, he definitely will.

Take every opportunity to be playful and friendly and have fun with people because in addition to meeting men, you might make a new girlfriend or just brighten some-one's day. When you do this, you'll feel happier in general because spreading warmth and kindness and all that good energy is contagious and makes the world a better place. So, go for it.

SAY CHEESE!

A couple of years ago, I was in New York City for a matchmaking industry conference. At the end of the day, I decided to walk from lower Manhattan all the way to my hotel in Midtown. The weather was beautiful, and I had just spent the day with my fun matchmaker friends. I was in a good mood, and I had a big smile on my face as I walked Uptown.

On the way back to my hotel, three different men stopped me to chat, and one of them asked me to go get a drink that afternoon. I'm no super model, and I wasn't dressed up in anything special, I was just smiling. I looked happy, and those guys felt comfortable saying "hi" because I looked like someone who'd be nice. When they stopped me, I thanked them for the compliment and let them know I was married. One guy said, "Your husband sure is a lucky guy!" I wasn't flirting one bit. I was just walking down the street on a lovely spring day with a big smile on my face. Sometimes, a smile is all it takes.

A few years back, a woman named Jane came to my office for an initial consultation. Jane was a tall slender blonde who, while attractive, looked rather plain. She arrived in my office wearing black pants, a black and white striped turtleneck, and her hair was tightly pulled into a ponytail. She wore no makeup. We talked for a while, and I asked her lots of questions so I could learn more about her to figure out exactly what was keeping her from meeting "the one." Jane, who was forty, told me that in her entire adult life, she'd never once been approached by a man, not in a bar or on the street, not at a coffee shop, not anywhere. I found that hard to believe. "No man has *ever* hit on you or asked you out?" I asked to make sure I'd heard her right. "Yes, that's right. It's never happened." When I hear something like this, especially from an attractive woman, my first thought is that she must be sending out a "do not talk to me" vibe without knowing it.

I asked Jane, "When's the next time you're going to be around single men you don't know?" She said, "I'm going to happy hour with some of my colleagues after work today." I asked if she could change her outfit into something a little more feminine, put on some makeup and do her hair before happy hour. "Nope, I'm going directly to the restaurant from my office, and I won't have time to change," she said.

It would've been better if she could have spruced herself up a little bit, but I decided to try an experiment regardless. I said, "Jane, tonight when you're at your happy hour, I want you to smile. When you're standing alone, I want you to smile so much that if someone sees you from across the bar, they'll wonder, *what the heck is she so happy about?* If someone is speaking to you, I want you to smile. And if you're talking, I want you to smile as well. I want you to smile so much that your face literally hurts tomorrow. Even if you feel stupid, just keep on smiling. Do we have a deal?" She agreed, we shook on it and finished up our meeting.

The next morning at 8:30 a.m. my phone rang. It was Jane, and she was excited. "You're not going to believe what happened last night! Two men asked me out, and they were the hottest guys in the bar! And one of them even told me I was the most approachable person in the whole place. I swear, he used those exact words. He said I was approachable!"

So, for the first time in her adult life, Jane, who was dressed in a striped turtleneck without any makeup on, was asked on dates by two attractive men, simply because she smiled. I love telling this story because it shows how clearly smiling can change your life. It's such an easy change to make, and if you practice, it'll become a habit. And smiling has a great side effect in addition to attracting men. Studies show that when you smile, you feel happier.

Pay attention to the vibe you put out to the world. Does your body language and energy say, "stay away" or does your smile say, "come on over"? When you smile, it's an invitation for men to talk to you. And it also makes you stand out. As you go through your day, look around. Do you see people smiling? Probably not. So, if you're walking down the street with a big smile on your face, you'll probably be the only one, and men will notice. Smiles are free, easy, and totally work. There's no invitation more enticing to a man. And if a man says hello to you, and you're not interested, please be kind. It takes courage to approach a woman, so cut him some slack. I hope you'll give smiling a try.

TAKE A CHANCE

Have you ever heard of a calling card? It's like a business card, except it's feminine and personal. I tell all of my female clients to get one because you never know when they'll come in handy. Years ago, when I was single, I had a calling card. It was red with a rose on it, and my name, phone number and email address were written in cursive – nothing more.

One day, I was sitting outside of the neighborhood Barnes and Noble with a friend, and we started chatting with a guy who was sitting on a bench next to us. He had a golden retriever with him, and his kids were running in and out of the bookstore, so I assumed he was married.

We talked for about ten minutes, and then my friend and I got up and left. As we were walking down the street, I told her I wished he was single. I said something like, "All the good ones are taken." And then she turned to me and said, "He's single. He told me he's been separated for over a year." "What?" I said. "You're telling me that hot guy on the bench with the dog is single? Oh my God, I have to go back!"

I ran back to the bookstore, and luckily, he was still sitting outside with his dog. I took my calling card out of my purse, and I walked up to him and said, "I have a gift for you. But don't look at it until I'm gone." I put the calling card in the front pocket of his shirt. Then, feeling a little embarrassed, I quickly walked away.

Five minutes later, my phone rang. It was the guy from the bookstore. His name was Tony, and I later found out he'd told my friend he was single because he was interested in me but too shy to make a move. "That was the coolest thing anyone's ever done," he said. And then he asked me out. Tony turned out to be a great guy. We dated for a while, and he wasn't "the one," but we had a lot of fun together.

Put down your phone, take off your EarPods, and connect with the people around you. Take a chance like I did and chat with a handsome stranger. You might meet someone wonderful and make a new friend or even fall in love.

DON'T BE A DATING DINOSAUR

Now, let's talk about dating online. About fifty percent of couples meet online, so if you're single and not dating using dating apps or websites, you're missing out on a real opportunity, and are, in essence, a "dating dinosaur." Gone are the days when people felt embarrassed that their friends might see them online. Everyone dates online now, and nobody cares. There are literally tens of thousands of age-appropriate single men online, and you can search for them from your couch in your pajamas with a glass of wine. What could be more convenient than that?

WHICH DATING SITE OR APP SHOULD YOU USE?

There are a lot of different sites and apps to choose from. Sites like Match.com (11 million), Plenty of Fish (150 million) and apps like Bumble (100 million) have millions of users and cater to pretty much everyone. Then there are niche sites and apps for smaller populations based on everything from religion to hobbies to eating habits. Yes, there are dating apps for Christians, dog lovers, vegetarians, athletes and Republicans. There are also dating sites for singles with disabilities. If you can dream it up, it probably exists. It doesn't matter which site or apps you use. They all have singles on them who are looking for love. I suggest you try two or three and see which ones work best for you.

BE STRATEGIC

Maybe you've dated online, and you hated it. If that's the case, I'm willing to bet you didn't have the right strategy. I'm going to share some things you can do to be more successful when dating online.

The most important part of your profile is your photos. They need to be excellent because men are so visual, and they're the first thing anyone sees. I suggest having a friend or even a photographer take photos of you specifically for your profile. When you have high quality photos, you're more likely to attract high quality men.

When you choose your photos:

- Wear colorful clothes and avoid big or busy patterns
- Avoid scarves and high necklines (it's a body language thing)
- Post five to six photos
- Your main profile should be a casual headshot (but not too close)
- You need at least one full-body photo
- Photos must be current and accurate
- Feel free to include fun activity photos (hiking, skiing, etcetera)
- Smile and look directly into the camera – no frowning or resting bitch face ;)
- No sunglasses
- No photos with groups of people
- Selfies are fine as long as they don't look like selfies
- Consider taking your photos outside; the lighting is better

When you write your profile, be playful, creative, and have fun with it. Write your essay in your own voice speaking directly to the reader. As a rule, show, don't tell. For example, share a fun and vivid story about a specific adventure you experienced instead of simply saying you're "adventurous." Don't be afraid to be specific; the details are what will make your profile stand out. And keep it 100 percent positive. Don't write *anything* negative. Remember, the man who's reading your profile is thinking, What's in it for me? What would my life be like if this woman was in it? So be warm, kind, funny and fun.

Please don't lie about *anything* on your profile. Put your correct age, your accurate body type, current photos, and include important information like the fact you have kids (I know someone who pretended she didn't have children, I swear it's true). For God's sake, be yourself. You're looking for a man who will love you, not some fictitious version of you.

If the site you're using allows you to hide your profile, use that feature so you don't get overwhelmed. I never let my clients have more than ten messages in their inbox at a time. This way they have the time to take a close look at each profile and to be kind and respond to everyone, even the men who aren't a fit. Taking things slowly and being curious about each person instead of making hasty assumptions is a good idea. Keep in mind that some wonderful men have bad profiles. Not everyone has a dating coach or a book like this to help them out. Try not to judge too harshly.

One-third of people who date online never go on a single date. That means there are a lot of men on dating sites and apps who will inevitably waste your time. When you connect with someone you like, don't message him forever. Instead meet him as soon as you've decided he seems normal and nice. The majority of men who date online and on dating apps are sincerely looking for a partner, so be grateful these amazing tools exists and can connect you with men who are looking for love.

Sometimes it takes a while to meet the right person, and that can be frustrating, but don't give up. My friend Susanna went on seventy-two Match.com dates, fell in love with number seventy, got married, had three kids, and lived happily ever after. Sometimes, dating is a numbers game, and you've got to be patient. I strongly suggest giving online dating a try and sticking with it.

If you just read the previous paragraph, and you're thinking, I don't care what Michelle says. I've tried online dating, and there aren't any quality men on there, the following story is for you.

My fifty-two-year-old client Regina told me she had a high-profile job and didn't feel comfortable dating online. After a lot of straight talk and some skillful cajoling (I basically told her to get over herself), I talked her into it. The irony is that on the same day her online profile went live, she was on the front page of the Huffington Post. I honestly hadn't realized how high-profile she was, and that's probably a good thing because of how things turned out.

I helped Regina pick out the right outfits – a couple of colorful fitted dresses and some skinny jeans with a red sleeveless top. She dyed her roots and had her hair blown out and her makeup done professionally. Then, I took Regina's photos and wrote a brand-new profile essay for her. I set everything up for her on Match.com and made her profile live. I posted her profile on a Friday and scheduled our next coaching call for three days later on the following Monday. That weekend, she was deluged with messages (I forgot to tell her to hide her profile). On Monday, she had about 150 emails in her inbox.

On our Monday call, I showed Regina the right way to read men's profiles and to write engaging messages. Then, I gave her some homework. I asked her to go through all of the messages on her own and to thoughtfully consider each one. I told her to delete the messages from men who definitely weren't a fit, respond to the ones who seemed interesting, and to save the mediocre profiles so we could go through them together.

On our next call, when we logged into Regina's Match.com account, her inbox was completely empty. Where did the 150 messages go? At that time, Match.com had a trash bin feature that saved deleted messages (they don't have it anymore). I checked the trash to see if the deleted messages were still there, and luckily, they were.

Confused, I asked Regina why she'd deleted all 150 emails. She said none of the men who'd messaged her were of a high enough caliber to be appropriate for her.

What?

Out of 150 men, there wasn't a single one she was open to meeting? Clearly, the problem wasn't the supply of men on Match, the problem was Regina. While Regina watched, I went into her trash bin and pulled out five men who looked interesting. I told her we were going to message them together, which we did. To make this long story short, Regina ended up marrying one of those five men. And the biggest irony is that he had a higher-level position in the current administration than she did. Over the years, I've pulled several husbands out of the trash. So be careful when you delete messages!

What I hope you learn from this story is that it's hard

to tell who the quality guys are online. Some great men have shitty profiles. And some shitty guys have great profiles. When you look at profiles, try to assume the best – not the worst – and give men a chance, even if their profiles are mediocre.

It's a good thing I met my husband at a restaurant. After we met, he showed me his online profile, and it was horrendous. The photos were abysmal, and he had written a bunch of negative stuff – all of the things he *didn't* want in a partner. Can you imagine? If he'd messaged me online, I would have rejected him. So, there it is. There are some good men behind some bad profiles, my wonderful husband included. I hope you'll keep that in mind when you give online dating a try.

How can you tell the difference between the quality commitment-minded men and the ones who will waste your time? The men who make an effort, write nice emails, share about themselves, ask you out and then follow through, those are the good guys. It's all about their effort and consistency. I also suggest you chat on the phone or on video before meeting anyone in person. A good guy won't mind making the extra effort because he'll want you to feel comfortable before meeting.

One last bit of online dating advice. Do not make negative assumptions. Don't assume men without photos are ugly or married. Maybe they have high-profile jobs and don't feel comfortable posting photos online. Ask them to send you photos so you can see who you're talking to. If you aren't attracted to the photos, politely decline. And don't assume men who are separated aren't ready to date. Instead, ask them how long they've been separated and if they're past the tough part yet. I've found that quality men, especially men in their forties and older, have a short shelf life. They get snapped up quickly, so don't wait until a man is officially divorced and then miss out. If there's something on a profile that could be a dealbreaker, I'd rather you ask about it than make an assumption and be wrong. The answer may surprise you.

ALWAYS BE SAFE

I would be remiss if I didn't remind you to always be careful. Tell a friend who you're meeting (take a screenshot) and set a specific time to call her when you get home. Meet your dates in public places so you don't put yourself at risk. If you don't feel comfortable, leave. Your safety should always be priority number one.

HAVE FUN

Most importantly, be playful and have fun when you date online. Dating is always supposed to be fun.

TRY SPEED DATING

Another great way to meet men is speed dating. It's an effective way to meet a lot of people in one sitting and quickly gauge chemistry to decide if you want to see them again. You'll typically sit in one spot and the men will rotate around the room. You get about five minutes to chat with each person, and then you decide who you'd like to connect with after the event. If the desire to meet is mutual, you'll receive each other's information. There are also companies that offer virtual speed dating events. Whether you attend via computer or go to a speed dating event in town, they're a great way to meet a variety of men. My clients often ask the best way to approach speed dating events. All you have to do is smile and be positive and friendly.

I went to my first speed dating event when I was forty-one. Most of the men I met that night were in their twenties. It was awkward, and to be honest, a waste of my time. I went with a couple of girlfriends, so at least we were together. Afterward, my friend Eve asked if I'd go to another speed dating event with her the following week. This one would be for singles older than thirty-five. Because I didn't have fun the first time, I declined. Eve ended up going by herself and wait for it... she met her husband. The moral of the story? Find an appropriate speed dating event for you. And if you don't have fun the first time you go, try it again. You never know who will show up.

EVEN MORE WAYS TO MEET MEN

Where else can you meet men? Google "singles events" in your area. Check out www.eventbrite.com to see what fun things are going on in your city or town. Join a Meetup group (www.meetup.com) and sign up for an activity you enjoy like a hike or a wine tasting where you can meet other singles while having fun. Most people go to Meetup events alone, so don't worry about arriving solo. Don't be afraid to put yourself out there. Worst case scenario, you'll have fun and make new friends. When you create your Meetup profile, use a clear attractive photo (without your cat). If you see someone you're interested in in your Meetup group, you can message them directly, so don't be surprised if a guy takes a chance and reaches out to you.

Don't be afraid to reach out to people on social media. I know a couple who met via Twitter. After commenting on each other's tweets, they took their communication offline. You can comment on Instagram posts or direct message men you're interested in. And don't be afraid to look at your friend's friends on Facebook. If someone looks interesting, ask them to connect you. Or reach out and private message the guy yourself. I'm not suggesting you repeatedly stalk people on social (please don't), but if you see someone interesting, there's no reason why you can't say hi to see if they're interested. Most men love when women reach out.

Lastly, don't forget one of your best resources, your friends and family who know and love you. Make sure everyone's aware you're ready to find a partner and you're open to being fixed up. Assure them that any fix up, no matter what the outcome, will be greatly appreciated.

You're looking for the man you're going to spend the rest of your life with. Don't be afraid to put yourself out there and take a chance. You've got to proactively make an effort. Either get out there and make an effort yourself or hire a matchmaker like me. Just like Nike says in their ads: Just do it!

10

DATE STRATEGICALLY

N ow that we've covered how to meet men, let's make sure you have fun, successful dates. We all know a bad first date can feel like torture, but a great first date can leave you walking on air. In this chapter, I'm going to cover everything you need to know to make sure your dates are fun and fruitful.

GETTING IN THE ZONE

Before you go on a date, it's important to cultivate the right kind of energy. If you're meeting someone during the week, leave your work energy behind and shift into your feminine energy before you meet. After work, go home and take some time to relax, change out of your work clothes and maybe light a candle and take a bubble bath or a hot shower. If you're going on a date directly after work, bring a change of clothes and take a few minutes to unwind before you shift gears.

GETTING READY

You need to show up looking your best for two reasons. First, I want you to look great for yourself. I want you to feel beautiful and confident so you can relax and enjoy yourself. Second, men are extremely visual, so how you look matters. Femininity is your superpower, so wear something feminine that makes you feel comfortable. I always recommend wearing color above the waist instead of black, gray, brown, navy or beige. When you wear color, you stand out. Look around and you'll see that almost everyone is wearing black. Also, studies show that when you wear color, you'll be perceived as more feminine, happier, kinder, more friendly and more open. Wear a dress if you feel like it. I've never heard a man complain because a woman wore a dress. I want you to walk into your date with a spring in your step because you know you look amazing.

SETTING YOUR INTENTION

How do you usually approach first dates? What's your goal, and what's your approach? If you're like most women, the first thing you look for is that instant "click" of physical attraction. Then you ask a lot of questions to figure out if the guy you're with could be the one for you. Do the two of you have a lot in common? Do you share the same values? Do you want the same things out of life? Are there dealbreakers? You assess and you judge. You try to figure things out quickly. You take all the information you've gathered and come up with a conclusion in about an hour and a half.

News flash – that's the wrong way to approach a first date. First of all, it's hard to feel a connection on a date when it's approached like an interview. And chemistry isn't something you have; it's something you create. I bet that's a concept you've never considered. I'll tell you more about that shortly.

BE IN THE MOMENT

Instead of trying to figure out if your date could be your future husband, what would happen if you simply decided to be in the moment and have a shared experience instead? Instead of worrying about the outcome, what if your only goal was to be yourself, have fun, learn all about the man you're with, see if you can get to the gooey center, to be kind and help him shine and have fun. If your goal is to be curious and have fun instead of what I call "qualifying the buyer" (figuring out if he might be your future husband), and you can stop worrying about next week, next year or happily ever after, the odds are you're going to have a much better experience. For the most part, people are pretty cool. And they often cross our paths for a reason.

You don't need to figure everything out so fast. At the end of a first date, the only thing you need to know is if you want to continue the conversation. A second date isn't a promise that you're going to date him or a declaration of anything important at all. It's simply an opportunity to get to know each other a little better, to talk some more. That's it. Unless someone *really* turns you off, you should go out again. In fact, I recommend meeting someone three times. It takes a while for some people to relax, unfold, and be themselves. It can take two or three dates to get a real feel for someone.

DECIDE TO HAVE FUN

For second and third dates, in addition to the typical drinks and dinner (I don't believe in coffee dates – they feel too platonic), I think creative activity dates are the way to go. Take a hike, go kayaking, visit a winery, take a dance class, hit some tennis balls, plan a picnic, go to a baseball game, play board games or sign up for a ghost tour. These activities are fun at any age. There are an infinite number of creative options and a lot of fun to be had.

Setting the intention to be fully present and to simply have fun on your dates is a wonderful gift to give yourself and the man you're with. There will be a lot less pressure on dates, and nothing creates connection more than feeling truly seen without being judged, and then having a fun experience together. Remember my client Miles, the violinist? If I could have fun with him – and I did – then you can have fun with just about anyone. Once you let go of judging and trying to figure things out and are genuinely curious instead, and especially if you're playful and have a positive attitude, you're going to enjoy your dates a hell of a lot more, I promise. When you stop analyzing and just have fun, you'll see that most people are pretty darn interesting and a lot of fun to be with.

MAKING CHEMISTRY HAPPEN

The way you start each date will influence the outcome. Before you arrive, I suggest you decide you're going to have a great time. Even if your energy is low after a long day at the office or with kids, try to arrive with a bright, positive amped up energy and as much enthusiasm as you can muster. The most important part of the date is the first five minutes. First impressions matter and impact what comes next. That's when you set the tone for the rest of the date, when you let your date know you're here to be present, to have fun, and that you like him already (even though you don't know him yet – you can decide later). Your first goal should be to make him feel liked right away. I try to do this with everyone I meet, not just when I was dating. It's such a kind thing to do.

When you're on a date, don't start with a handshake. I tell my clients to greet their date with a warm hug, then give him the biggest smile you've got and say something nice, like:

- It's so awesome to finally meet you
- It's so nice to meet you, I've been looking forward to our date
- _____ (the person who set you up) said so may nice things about you

And if you love to flirt:

- Wow, you're even more handsome than your photos
- When I saw you standing over there, I thought to myself, "I really hope that's my date" (and then smile)

When you greet your date, that hug, smile and positive comment translate to: "I'm happy to be here," and, "I like you already." Which feels good, and helps a man relax and just be himself. It's a great way to start the date. Then, when you get to the table, the bar, or wherever you meet, make a second positive comment, like:

- Wow, you picked a nice place, great job
- This place is really cool
- This was such a fun idea, I'm glad you thought of it

I'm sure his ex-girlfriend or his ex-wife spent plenty of time telling him everything he did wrong. What a lovely gift to let him know he's doing great so far. So, take off those dating goggles and look for what's right. And when you notice something you like about him, don't just think it, say it. If you're thinking, Wow, he seems like a great dad, instead of keeping it to yourself say, "I can tell by the way your face lights up when you talk about your son that you're a wonderful dad." What a nice thing to say to make him feel truly seen and appreciated.

When you do share your appreciation out loud, men will relax and show up even more authentically. It's human nature to like people who like us and to open up when we feel appreciated and accepted. You're creating a safe space for him to relax and be himself. That's a nice thing to do. And it'll make the date not only more enjoyable, but more connected too.

THE QUESTION

When I ask women, "What's the one thing that will make a man decide he wants to see you again?" I get a lot of different answers but usually not the correct one. Contrary to what many women think, although looking great does help, it's not how you look that makes men want to go out again. The reason most men want to spend more time with you is the way you make them feel. The way you make them feel about *themselves*, to be more specific. Men are wonderfully uncomplicated. If you make them feel good, they'll want more of that feeling. It's as easy and simple as that.

LIKE HIM FIRST

On dates, men typically look for signals from women to see if we're interested. They try to figure out if we like them by looking for clues. And while they look for clues, we wait for a sign they're into us. So, basically, both people wait, and nobody feels liked, so no one relaxes, leans in or has fun. When this happens, it's a missed opportunity and such a shame.

I suggest you act like you like him first, before you actually decide if you do. Doing that is both kind and strategic. You'll put him at ease, and you'll have a much more enjoyable and connected experience if you do. You can decide later if you want another date. For now, just be super nice, and help him shine.

CAN ATTRACTION GROW?

What if you meet a guy, and you're not that attracted to him, should you still act enthusiastic on the date? Of course. For most women, attraction can grow when a man is brilliant or funny or talented or especially kind. Take the time to find out who he is and what makes him unique; find his gooey center. Worst case, if he's not a romantic fit, you'll make a new friend or just make him feel good while you're together. Being kind is always a win.

HAVING GOOD CONVERSATIONS

During the date, keep the conversation on positive subjects. Don't ask about his ex and why they broke up. And if he asks you, quickly give him the basics, and then give that subject a pass. Don't talk about politics and pandemics and such. Rather, talk about what you love, what makes you happy, what makes you enthusiastically you. And when you ask questions about him, listen to his answers. Don't skip from question to question quickly moving on from, "What do you do for fun" to "Where's your favorite place to travel?" Listen to his answers, go deeper, learn more. If you are genuinely curious about what makes him tick, you'll have more fun and connect on a deeper level than if you're just trying to figure out if he passes the test, if he's the one for you.

HELP A GOOD GUY OUT

We've all been on a date with a guy who talks about himself all night long or peppers you with exhausting questions. Remember, *some good guys are bad at dating.* The next time you're on a date, and the guy's doing something that's making you think, He's probably not for me, instead of shutting down, help him out. If he's talking about negative subjects, point that out, and ask to keep the conversation happier. If he's talking too much, thank him for being so open and ask him what he'd like to know about you. If he's asking too many questions, thank him for making an effort to learn about you, then tell him it's his turn to share. Instead of writing someone off and going through the motions for the rest of the date, see if you can turn the date around by skillfully maneuvering in a helpful way. You might end up having a much better time than you expected.

MY CLIENT, WILLIAM: THE TALKER

I had a brand-new client named William. He was such a nice guy, a loving and involved father of two young kids, who had been divorced for several years. This was his first foray into dating, so for his first introduction, I matched him with a friend of mine. I did that for two reasons. First, because she was exactly the kind of woman he asked to meet. But more importantly, because I trusted her and knew she'd tell me honestly what he was like. It's not only my job to find the right match for my clients, but I also help them make a good impression. Feedback is important, and I knew my friend Melissa would be helpful.

After their date, I called William first. He was excited. "Michelle, you're so good at what you do. Melissa was amazing. She was smart, interesting and beautiful. We were together for four hours. It was an incredible date. Thank you!"

I was excited. I thought I'd hit a homerun. Until later when I spoke with Melissa who said, "Oh my God, that was four hours of total hell for me. You seriously owe me, girlfriend."

What?

She said, "He literally talked about himself for four straight hours. I swear to God, he did not ask me a single question about myself. I was nice to him because he's your client, but you need to coach him, Michelle. He was horrible." I thanked her profusely for meeting him and for being so honest, then I called him up and told him exactly what she said.

At first, William was mortified, but then he laughed. "You know what? She's absolutely right. Now that I think about it, I did talk too much. Honestly, it's been a long time since I had someone other than my kids to talk with. I guess I need to get out more," he laughed.

Isn't it interesting that William thought Melissa was "smart and interesting" given the fact he didn't ask her anything about herself? Sometimes listening, which is what Melissa did, is all it takes to make a man feel good. Obviously, there has to be more give and take than that, but it's interesting to note. Too bad Melissa didn't know how to help him out and turn the date around. Instead, she just sat through it, miserable, as a favor to me.

MY CLIENT, WILLIAM: THE LISTENER

After I coached William on the phone, I set him up with another woman who I thought he'd like. I told him he was not allowed to talk more than forty percent of the time. A quick learner, he did exactly as I instructed, and his second match liked him a lot. She actually wrote on her feedback survey that he was, and I quote, "a good listener." When I read that, I literally laughed out loud. I called William up to share her feedback, and we both had a good laugh. You see, some great guys do need a little help. All William needed was a little bit of coaching, and he caught right on. If you run into a guy who talks too much, I hope you'll help him out.

THE DUMB-DUMB

But what do you do with the guy who just doesn't get it? The bore, the bragger, the incessant talker, the annoying guy who you know you just don't like. If you've tried to help him out, and he's just not catching on, be kind, finish the date, and then move on. You can't help everyone. Some people are beyond help and going on a shitty date once in a while is just par for the course. But don't worry, they're not a waste of time. The Universe sees how hard you're trying. And you're learning every time you meet someone. Hopefully, there will be many more good dates than bad ones, especially if you learn to skillfully navigate and help men shine. It sounds like a lot of work, but the more you do it, the easier, more natural, and more fun it will get. Dating is a skill. The more you practice, the better at it you'll get, and the more fun you'll have.

WHO SHOULD PAY?

I'm in my fifties and a little old fashioned, so my feeling is, if a man asked you out, he should pay. But my daughters are in their late twenties and tell me their friends prefer to go Dutch. Whatever makes you feel comfortable is what you should do. However, please don't offer to split the check if you are going to be disappointed when he takes you up on your offer. If you do that, you're setting him up to fail. Only offer if you are one hundred percent fine paying for yourself. If you asked him out and invited him on the date, that's another story. Then you should treat, although he'll probably want to pay or at least split the bill.

If the gentleman does pay, thank him like he's never been thanked before. I tell my clients to thank their date three times: when he pays, when you get up from the bar or table, and again when you part ways. From the feedback I've gotten from men after dates, it's interesting to note that sometimes they won't hear a casual, "thank you." So, if someone is kind enough to treat you to a lovely dinner or even just a drink, make sure he's knows how much you appreciate his generosity. Dating can get expensive. He wants to know that you genuinely appreciated his efforts.

HOW TO END A DATE

Just like the first five minutes matter, the way you end your dates is important too. This is when the man is working particularly hard to read you to see if you want to go out again. He's looking for a greenlight, so he knows he can ask you out again. This is often where things go wrong, and signals get crossed or misread.

Men experience a lot of ghosting and rejection from woman who say "sure, I'd love to go out again" when they don't mean it. If you had a good time and want to see him again, don't suggest getting together again. That's his job. But do tell him you had an awesome time. Be exceedingly enthusiastic and say something like, "That was even more fun than I thought it would be!" or "Wow, I had so much fun with you!" or "You're so much fun to be with, that was a blast, thank you!" If you like him, make sure he knows without a doubt that your "yes" means yes. He needs to know you'll say "yes" if he asks you out again.

WHAT IF YOU'RE NOT INTERESTED?

What should you do if you don't like him? Thank him and say it was nice meeting him. If he asks you out again, you can decline on the spot if you feel comfortable. Or you can say "sure" and then send him a note later letting him know you've thought about it, and even though he's a great guy, you just don't feel the two of you are a fit. Don't leave him hanging. Send the note within twenty-four hours.

NO GHOSTING

The one thing you should never do is to ghost someone. Ghosting is when you don't respond or when you disappear. I know it's hard to let someone down, but being honest and direct is actually a kind thing to do. It gives closure so people can move on and not waste their time or be confused. Being honest and kind is always the way to go. Even though it's hard to let someone down, remember when you're kind, your dating karma grows. Yes, that's a thing. Plus, being kind feels good. Some men will even thank you for letting them know.

THE "THANK YOU" TEXT

Should you send a "thank you" text after a date or just wait to see if he texts or calls? Whether or not you send a text is entirely up to you. If you ended your date with enthusiasm like I described, you don't need to follow up by text, but you can if you want to. Just remember to always play poker. Once you've given a date your all and made it clear you're interested, he knows where to find you. If he doesn't follow up, forget he exists and put your energy into someone else. Remember, you are the dream job. If he doesn't feel it's the right job for him, why on earth would you want to hire him? Keep moving down the football field toward your future husband. Don't let anyone waste your time or get in your way.

SHOULD YOU GO ON A SECOND DATE?

In my career as a matchmaker, I've listened to feedback after literally thousands of dates, and it always amazes me how interesting, and sometimes unpredictable or even downright weird, the feedback can be. Sometimes couples just click, the conversation flows, and there's instant chemistry. It's so awesome when that happens. But sometimes dates flop, and there's no connection at all. That's just par for the course. You can't connect with everyone you meet. While we all want to feel that instant chemistry, fireworks even, the reality is that most of the time, the dates you go on will be just okay – pretty good, but not amazing. Perhaps you'll have a nice time, but he won't "wow" you. After dates like this, you might be on the fence or even decline. However, when a date is just so-so, I always recommend going out again.

I had a client named James a few years back. He was a handsome forty-something attorney who had just moved to DC after an amicable divorce. His first introduction was to my client, Claire. I had a strong feeling they'd like each other, and so I made the match. After the two of them met, James filled out his post-date feedback survey indicating he did not want to go out with Claire again. But Claire had a great time. She liked James.

I called James to see if I could move the needle. She was attractive, smart, and successful. James agreed that Claire had all the qualities on his list, but he just didn't see himself with "someone like her." I listened to him explain then told him she wanted to see him again. I pointed out the obvious. "James, you're new to town. It's not like you have a busy social calendar. I introduced you to a quality woman who's into you. Just go on one more date with her, and if you're still not feeling it, maybe you'll make a friend."

It took a bit of cajoling, but James finally agreed to a second date with Claire, and I'm glad he did. They're now married with an adorable one-year-old daughter. Sometimes, well-meaning nudges from your matchmaker are necessary. But what if you don't have a matchmaker like me to nudge you when you're wrong? What if you judge too quickly and opt out with men you should give a chance to?

Over the years, I've convinced dozens of clients to go on second dates when they didn't want to or were on the fence, and many ended up together. Almost everyone has blind spots when they're dating, and it's my job to make sure my clients don't miss out on someone special. They don't always listen, but I try. What if you have blind spots just like James did? I'm willing to bet you do.

SHOULD YOU GO ON A SECOND DATE?

There are four questions you should ask yourself to decide if you should go on a second date.

1. Was there at lease some level of attraction? You don't have to think he's super-hot. We're looking for an attraction level of about six (or higher).
2. From what you can tell, is he a good person?
3. Did you enjoy spending time with him?
4. Were there any obvious undeniable dealbreakers? If you want to have kids, and he doesn't, that's a dealbreaker. If you want to stay in your current city, and he's moving to France next Thursday, unless you're a Francophile, that's a dealbreaker as well.

If you answered "yes" to questions one, two and three and "no" to question four, a second date is definitely in order.

BUT IT'S HARD

Dating can be a lot of fun, but sometimes dating is just hard. If you feel frustrated, know that you're not alone. I'll never forget crying in the shower and all the other times I felt sad. Most of my clients feel frustrated at one time or another. At the end of the day, dating is a means to an end, and I assure you, if you stick with it, make a consistent effort and utilize the strategies in this book, you *will* be successful. But there may be times when you need to take a break, and that's okay. Give yourself the time you need to reenergize and start again.

MY CLIENT, LISA

Lisa was a fairly anxious dater who had previously had some bad experiences with dating and with men. At thirty-seven, she was determined to find her husband and to fulfill her dream of becoming a mother. She felt time was running out, so she had recently frozen her eggs.

What I loved about working with Lisa was her determination to get as much from our coaching as she could and then to implement what she'd learned. After each call, she'd send me a bullet point list of everything I'd taught her. It was quite something. She also kept an Excel spreadsheet detailing all of her efforts and dates. There was a line with each man's name. There was a column for the men she talked with on the phone. There was a column for men she ended up meeting. She kept track of every relationship, how long it lasted, when it ended, and who ended it – her or him.

She analyzed her dates as she progressed, which was

brilliant. I would be lying if I said everything went smoothly. There was the time Lisa called me crying because some asshole she'd cooked a beautiful dinner for dumped her when she wouldn't sleep with him (good for her). But she stuck with it.

A month or so after our work together, she met a man named Noah. When she told me he was getting up early to drive into the city to run with her three mornings a week, I knew he was into her. He sounded like a great guy.

Fast forward about a year, I found myself on an airplane headed to Knoxville, Tennessee, where I had the pleasure of attending their wedding. Over cocktails, we reminisced about her Excel spreadsheet. Noah was number forty-two. She had gone on dates with forty-two men to find "the one." I told her she should frame that spreadsheet for old times' sake.

Lisa thanked me. She said she never would have met Noah if she hadn't worked with me. You see, he's older than she is, and he has four kids. Before I coached her, she only dated men close to her age who weren't dads. Thank goodness she opened up her search and found such a wonderful man. She got pregnant on their honeymoon, and now they have the most beautiful little girl. I love going to her birthday parties each year.

DO NOT GIVE UP

This cartoon says it all, and I often show it to my clients if they're feeling discouraged. Just like everything else you've pursued and accomplished in your life, if you're determined and don't give up, even when it's frustrating or hard, you will be successful. Be like Lisa. Cry, and then get back to work. Learn everything you can learn, get help if you need it, and then do not give up. When I think of her, I always smile.

GETTING CENTERED

Lastly, if you're going to muster all that energy and put your best foot forward, take off those dating goggles and do your best to connect with your date's gooey center, that may require a little inspiration. I've found it's helpful to get centered before each date with a short metta meditation. A metta (love) meditation is a truly beautiful thing. You may want to try this before your dates.

Take some time before your date to sit quietly for ten minutes (or longer if you wish). Sit so you're comfortable but erect. You can put your hands over your heart if you want to, close your eyes, and then quietly focus on your breath. Breathe in and out slowly and deeply. If your mind wanders, notice that without judgment, and then bring your attention back to your breath. Now, as your mind quiets, connect with your intention for happiness, ease, and safety by silently repeating:

> *"May I be safe.*
> *May I be peaceful.*
> *May I be happy.*
> *May I be well.*
> *May I be at ease."*

Then, think about the man you're about to spend time with. Even though you may not know this person, send him your positive energy and love. He's also looking for love, so your hope for him is that he can enjoy your time together. You also hope that he is happy, whatever that looks like for him. Offer this loving-kindness meditation to connect with him even before you meet. Cultivate your intention of kindness and offer your date a few phrases of love.

> *"May you be safe.*
> *May you be peaceful.*
> *May you be happy.*
> *May you be well.*

May you be at ease."

Finally, before you finish, send your loving-kindness as a wish for the whole world.

"May we all be safe.
May we all be peaceful.
May we all be happy.
May we all be well.
May we all be at ease."

Sit for a while longer and focus on the rise and fall of your chest. Be aware of the feeling of love and kindness you've cultivated in your heart and your whole body. Sit peacefully with that feeling.

And then, when you feel ready, you can end your meditation and go have a kickass date.

11

DECIDE IF HE'S "THE ONE"

W e've come a long way together, and I've given you a lot of information to digest and absorb. We've covered how to meet men, how to be strategic and how to have successful dates. We've also covered how to get clear on what your needs are versus your preferences as well as how to have strong boundaries and advocate for yourself. I hope you've taken the time to write down your list of needs and your protective contract. These are the tools you'll use when you're dating from now on. Whether you're dating someone new or if you have an exclusive boyfriend, please continue to look at your list of needs and protective contract regularly to make sure your needs are being met and there are no red flags.

Despite all you've learned, men are still confusing, and change can be tough, so I've written a checklist you can use to figure out if the guy you're dating is genuinely interested in having a relationship with you. If he's doing all twelve of these things, the odds are he's smitten.

TWELVE WAYS TO TELL IF A GUY LIKES YOU

1. He stays in touch every single day.

When a guy likes you, he wants to hear your voice or see your name pop up in his text messages. Even on the days you don't see each other, he checks in to say "hi" and let you know you're on his mind.

2. He tells you what he likes about you.

You don't have to wonder if he likes you because he tells you that he does. He consistently pays you compliments. What a nice guy.

3. He calls when he says he'll call.

No more sitting by the phone waiting for him to call. He calls exactly when he says he will, so you don't have to feel anxious. You know you can depend on him.

4. He asks to spend time with you (consistently and often).

A man who's excited about you will do more than just text or call. He'll make sure he spends lots of time with you on a regular basis (no matter how busy he is).

5. He asks you out in advance.

You don't have to sit around wondering if you're going to see him this weekend. He asks you out in advance, and you've got a date on your calendar. If a guy likes you, he'll pin you down and make sure you're on his calendar (instead of on some other guy's calendar).

6. He plans real dates.

He doesn't just ask you to hang out at his place (or yours) with Netflix and a pizza (although that's fun once in a while). He plans real dates (like dinner, drinks, theater, museums, hikes, day trips and more) because he wants to have fun with you.

7. He makes an effort.

When a guy likes you, he makes an effort. He texts, calls, plans dates, picks you up and may even pick up the check. He doesn't mind working a little harder because he feels you're worth the effort.

8. He doesn't make you feel anxious (at all).

He makes you feel "comfortable," and you can be yourself around him. You never have to worry about whether or not you'll hear from him because he's consistent and makes you feel secure. You feel relaxed around him instead of anxious.

9. He goes out of his way to spend time with you (even when he's busy).

He doesn't give you a lame excuse for why he can't see you this week. Even if work is crazy, he's got errands or he's got a marathon to train for, he finds time for you. He makes sure he sees you no matter what else is going on in his life because he cares about you and enjoys being with you.

10. He introduces you to his peeps.

He wants his friends (and eventually his family) to meet you. And he wants to see how you get along with the people in his life because he's figuring out if you're a long-term fit.

11. He's fine waiting to have sex.

When a man really likes you, he'll wait. Even though he's attracted to you and would love to be intimate, he respects your boundaries and waits until you're ready (which should be after he asks you to be his girlfriend).

12. He asks you to be exclusive and date only him.

After the two of you have been dating for a while, he asks you to be exclusive. He wants you to be his girlfriend and stop dating other men (and if he's doing all of the above, I hope you'll say "yes!").

In this modern digital age of dating-overload-and-too-many-options, men don't have to work hard to find a date. But to find love, they'll happily make an effort. Remember, stop focusing on what men say and watch what they do. If the guy you're dating does the things on the list above, he's probably interested in landing the dream job. You deserve a man who's excited about you.

HOW CAN YOU TELL IF HE'S "THE ONE?"

I teach my clients that the fastest way to find the right man is to end things with the wrong man right away. But sometimes it's hard to know if you should stay or let go. Especially if the guy you're dating has great qualities and you care about him. To make things a little less confusing for you, I've put together a list of fifteen questions to ask yourself when you're trying to figure out if the man you're dating is the right person for you. Take your time, carefully consider each question, and be thoughtful about your answers.

1. Is the relationship easy and enjoyable at least 95 percent of the time?
2. Can I trust my partner 100 percent?
3. Can I be myself with him?
4. Is he consistently kind?
5. Do we share similar values (or if our values differ slightly, can we respectfully agree to disagree and make it work?)
6. Do we have similar life goals?
7. Does my partner love and respect me exactly as I am?
8. Do I respect my partner exactly as he is?
9. Do we have fun together?
10. Is my partner supportive of my dreams and endeavors?
11. Do we communicate openly, thoughtfully and honestly?
12. Do I love touching him?

13. If you have kids: Is this union in the best interest of my children?
14. Do I feel comfortable and at ease in this relationship?
15. Do I feel happy in general while in this relationship?

If you answered, "yes" to all fifteen questions, you've probably got a keeper on your hands.

If you answered "no" to any of the questions above, you may be wasting valuable time. Do not invest in someone who isn't fully invested in you. And don't ever stay in an unsatisfying, stressful, hurtful or abusive relationship. The right relationship will take some work, but it won't be hard. The right relationship will enhance your happiness, not deplete it. It takes strength to keep the promise you've made to yourself. You can end things. You can do this. But how exactly?

BREAKING UP

Once you've realized he isn't your husband, end things right away. Why waste more valuable time? As a rule of thumb, I suggest you take the following steps to let him go kindly and decisively:

1. Thank him for all of the time he's spent with you and for the generosity he's shown
2. Pay him several genuine compliments. Even though he's not for you, he's still a good guy (if he's an asshole, skip steps one and two)

3. Let him know you've decided the two of you are not a long-term fit
4. Wish him well

It's as simple as that.

Every situation is different and ending things after a few weeks isn't the same as ending them after several months, so please do what feels right to you. But whether the relationship is fairly new or if it's longer-term, be decisive, cut the connection and then move on. When you do that, you'll open space in your life for the right man to fill. Keep on moving down the football field toward "the one."

However, if you answered "yes" to the questions above, and you think he could be "the one," then woo hoo, I'm so happy for you! Don't ever stop checking your list of needs and protective contract. Relationships should not be hard, but they do need tending. Make sure you tend your garden every single day.

RELATIONSHIPS ARE LIKE GARDENS

I've always loved the analogy, "relationships are like gardens." To have a beautiful garden, you must tend to it each day. It's nice to be outside in the garden enjoying the soil and the sun. When you see a weed, you pull it. When a bush needs trimming, you trim it. It isn't hard to do.

But what if you neglect your garden, and it grows unchecked? You'll end up with a weedy mess. When you finally get around to taking care of it, you'll have to pull tons of weeds, trim overgrown bushes, get scratched by thorns, bitten by bugs – you get the picture.

Just like a garden, your relationship will need daily maintenance in the form of consistent honest and open communication. It will require patience, and sometimes even forgiveness. When you and your partner decide to have a conscious relationship and to nurture your garden together, you'll build a union that works, one that lasts. I hope you'll commit to growing a beautiful garden with your partner.

HOW SHOULD THE RIGHT RELATIONSHIP FEEL?

The right relationship will feel like warm chocolate chip cookies and your favorite pair of jeans, comfortable and delicious. When you're with the right man, you'll feel safe, relaxed, and at home. I don't know many couples who have passionate sex on the dining room table after twenty years of marriage. But I do know couples who are there for each other through the good times and the bad. It's not about fireworks and Hollywood sex scenes. It's about building and sharing a life with someone you love, your best friend, a man you can count on, who adores you, who's got your back.

If you utilize the lessons and tools I've taught in this book, make a consistent effort, stay positive and have faith, you will inevitably find the one.

AVOIDING THE ROADBLOCKS
AHEAD

Since you've made it this far, you have a lot of information to digest and a lot of new strategies to put into place. I know how much finding your partner means to you, and I want to make sure you find him soon. But wanting to find your partner and knowing exactly what you need to do doesn't mean you'll follow through. Completely changing your approach to dating and relationships is a big undertaking and doing things in a new way can be hard.

The Universe is ready to send you the right man, but if you get stuck in the wrong relationship again and aren't available, you'll be right where you started before reading this book. I want you to stay on track. I want you to find your guy. To make sure you succeed, I suggest you find someone to hold you accountable so you don't slip into old habits. Having a friend, mentor or a coach at the ready to make sure you utilize the lessons in this book and stay on track is something I strongly recommend.

STAYING ON TRACK

I've had this book you're reading inside my head for many years. I started to write it more than a dozen times, but every time I tried, I got sidetracked or didn't have the discipline to get the job done. I failed so many times, I felt bad about myself. I thought, So many other people have written books; why the hell can't I make it happen? Thinking it would help, I bought several books about writing non-fiction. Even though I read them all, I still didn't write the book. I was always too busy or had some other reason why I couldn't get it done.

When the pandemic hit, I had more free time on my hands. I knew it was the right time to write, but I was afraid I'd fail again. And to be honest, with everything going on in the world, I needed a win, something to feel good about. I'd failed to finish so many times, I knew I had to hire a coach to get it done. I was determined to write this book.

In the end, I didn't only hire a coach. I hired an entire team to walk me through the process. I had a coach to teach me and keep me on track, an editor to help me write, and a graphic artist to design my book cover. I even joined a Facebook group with other writers, so I had a community of likeminded people to turn to for help. Before I typed a single word, I had all the support I needed in place.

Even with all the enlisted help, I still slipped into old habits. When I made excuses about not having enough time, my coach gave me a to-do list with specific instructions and due dates for each part of the book. She even said if I didn't get my chapters in on time, she wouldn't work with me anymore. I had no choice but to get them written on time. When self-doubt crept in, my community of writers was there to cheer me on and kept me inspired. And when I wasn't sure if my writing was good enough, my editor had my back.

After so many years of dreaming about being an author and wanting to use my expertise to help women like you stop wasting time and finally find love, I did it. I wrote every word in this book with you in my heart, and I could not have gotten it done without all that support. It feels amazing to have finally accomplished my goal and to be able to help you find your love.

I'm a high achiever who's accomplished many things in my life, but this darn book was hard for me to get done. Now that it's finished, I couldn't be more thrilled. And even though I had tons of support, I'm taking all the credit. I feel like a huge weight has been lifted. I have a message to share, and I'm sharing it with you. I'm so grateful I did what it took to reach my goal.

Sometimes, even high achievers like you and me need help doing and seeing things differently. We might need a new strategy, or a deeper understanding of how things work or a second set of eyes that can give us an entirely new perspective to help us reach our goals. I believe it's a sign of strength, not weakness, to ask for help when you need it. I got the help I needed to write this book, and here you are reading it (yay). I hope you'll consider doing whatever it takes to reach your goals too. If you can do it on your own, go for it. But if you need help and guidance, please get the support you need.

FIND THE RIGHT SUPPORT

Years ago, I took some bad advice from a girlfriend that kept me in the wrong relationship for years. I don't know why I listened to her. Looking back, she was ill-equipped to offer advice since her marriage wasn't all that great. I wasted years in that relationship when I could have moved on. My friend was sincerely trying to help, but it was a case of the blind leading the blind.

Whatever you do, don't listen to the wrong people. Don't take advice from your single friends who haven't found love yet or from coupled friends who don't have the kind of relationship you ultimately want to have. Your friends love you, but that doesn't mean they know the right way for you to date. Be careful when you choose your support. Make sure you find the right person, someone with experience who's been successful in love, to keep you on track.

FIND THE TIME

Most of my clients are busy businesswomen who work hard, love to travel and have busy social lives. If that sounds like you, please slow down to make dating a priority, and do everything I've suggested in this book. If you know altering your busy schedule to make this a priority is going to be a challenge, you'll need a system and support to keep you on track.

Be aware of what gets in your way. Notice the ways you sabotage yourself. Do you work too much because work is your comfort zone? Do you avoid dating because it makes you feel anxious? Is the fast pace of your life keeping you so busy you don't have time to date or develop a deeper relationship?

If you know you're not going to walk the walk, find an accountability partner, a friend or a coach who can keep you on track. Together, block out time on your calendar to devote to dating and have them hold you to it. You need to stop being so busy, make time, push through the anxiety, and make finding your partner your number one priority. If you don't make time to do what it takes, nothing will change.

STEPPING OUTSIDE OF YOUR COMFORT ZONE

One of my favorite mantras is "the best things in life happen outside of your comfort zone." When I tried writing my book on my own, I got super stressed out. To alleviate my anxiety, I tried everything from eating, taking breaks, to reading about writing instead of actually doing it. None of those things made me feel any better or helped me get the job done. I wasn't able to step outside of my comfort zone until I had support.

I'm asking you to date differently than you've dated in the past. And doing things differently will probably make you anxious. Dating is stressful no matter how you slice it, even when you have a book like this to help you. If feelings come up for you, stop and get centered. There are a gazillion meditation apps you can download. Use them. Slow down, breathe and calm yourself. Then take it one step at a time. Find a community of single women who can support you. If it works for you, find a coach who can help you every step of the way. Please don't let anxiety stop you from reaching your goal. You have to push through discomfort to get to the other side, and I know you can.

TRUST THE PROCESS

Even if you follow every single piece of advice in this book, it will probably take time to find "the one." You may get discouraged along the way and doubt what you've learned here. You may be tempted to go back to your old way of doing things. That may feel good at first, but you'll get the same results you got before.

Please trust the process I'm teaching you and know it's normal to get frustrated or even discouraged. The majority of my clients were frustrated at one point. Dating, by design, is frustrating. But when my clients finally met "the one," and their dating days were behind them, they were glad they hung in there and didn't give up. You will be too.

Dating is a means to an end. Keep your mind focused on your goal, and have faith that the strategies in this book will get you there. What I've taught you worked for me, and it's worked for hundreds of my clients. Trust the process and never ever give up. You will meet your husband when the time is right.

LET GO

Smart successful women like you are used to setting goals and then getting shit done. You set a goal, you work hard, and you succeed.

And then there's dating...

When you're dating, no matter how hard you work, no

matter how much you prepare, and no matter how much you want to, you cannot control the outcome. So, please stop trying. If you try to control things, you're going to fail. You need to be open to whatever comes. I've given you the tools to assess every situation. Please make sure you use them.

If you don't actually write your protective contract and list of needs, you won't be able to put them to use. If you don't play poker and instead try to run the show, the odds are you'll end up with the wrong guy again. If you think having sex early on is going to make things move along faster, I assure you, you're making a mistake.

To be successful, you're going to have to trust this process and stop trying to control the outcome. Stop worrying about the future and enjoy the ride right now. Because if you continue to push a square peg into a round hole harder and harder, it still won't fit. Stop pushing. Let go and trust this process, and everything will be okay.

STOP JUDGING

When I work with my one-on-one clients, I teach them the same things I've taught you in this book. I ask them not to be judgmental and to realize that sometimes good men are bad at dating. And yet, when we log into their Match.com inboxes together, without fail, they've elimi- nated good men. It drives me crazy.

I don't know why some women have such a hard time taking off their dating goggles. If you find yourself stuck in judgment and you're making assumptions, you're going to miss out on someone great. Do you remember my high-profile client Regina who deleted her entire inbox because she thought no one was good enough? Thank goodness I was there to pull her husband out of the trash. Left to her own devices, she'd still be single instead of happily married.

It's important to be curious about the possibilities instead of making false assumptions. Most of your judgments and assumptions are wrong. As I always say, "Assumptions keep you single." Open your heart and your mind and try something new.

DON'T LET YOUR EGO CHOOSE FOR YOU

One of my biggest frustrations as a matchmaker is working with people who cannot get their egos out of their way. In this book, I've asked you to go deeper, and to look for someone who meets your emotional needs, adores you and treats you right. How tall, wealthy or educated a man is will have no impact on his ability to be a good partner. Looking for these shallower things is not a smart strategy and may stop you from finding the one.

Don't choose a man because you look good together or because people expect you to date someone like him. If you find yourself thinking, I deserve a tall, handsome, rich, PhD, catch yourself, and stop it. Don't fall into old habits and focus on qualities that don't matter. Stay focused on the gooey center, the kindness, the values, the heart of the man. That's the smartest way to find a healthy and lasting relationship. Follow the steps I've outlined in this book, and you'll see. When you finally find a man who treasures you and loves you the way you deserve to be loved, you'll realize how trivial things like height and income are. I assure you, having a man who loves you right will be worth the compromise.

THE BRIGHT, SHINY OBJECT

It's inevitable that you're going to meet a man who excites you. It's happened before, and it'll happen again. He may be handsome, sexy and have everything on your list. The guy who seems perfect may be the "bright shiny object" who will distract you from dating according to plan. He may turn out to be amazing, but he may also be "fool's gold." Be careful.

Don't let your excitement trick you into letting down your guard and forget the tools I've given you. Don't ignore red flags because you're an optimist and see his potential, that's not wise. There's a reason for the saying, "love is blind." Don't let your endorphins steal the show.

Don't sweep red flags under the rug ever again. Use your protective contract to address them and move on if need be. No matter how sexy he is or how perfect he looks on paper, if he's not treating you right, meeting your needs, and showing you consistently that he's into you, you need to move on. A lot of women who read this book are going to mess up here. Don't be one of them. Follow the strategies I teach.

ADDICTED TO DRAMA

If you grew up in a tumultuous home where there was fighting, yelling or other similar behavior, you're more likely than most to gravitate toward drama in your relationships because drama is your normal. If this is true for you, dating a man who is "nice" may seem boring at first. Please be careful not to let him go too soon. If nice feels boring, sit with it for a while. When I met my husband, he was so easygoing and available, it felt a little weird at first. But after a while, I got used to the lack of drama. I've got to be honest; it was quite a relief.

Sometimes drama feels exciting. Don't fall into that trap. Use the lists in Chapter 11 to determine if a relationship is healthy for you. Your past doesn't have to control your future. You have the power to do things differently and to get comfortable with what is healthy. If you feel stuck in drama, you might want to seek out a counselor or a coach to help you move past your old ways.

IF IT GETS HARD, REBOOT, AND KEEP ON GOING

When dating gets hard, don't make the same old excuses you've made in the past. If your old belief system creeps back in, stop and reread this book. If you're having trouble staying positive and on track, find support, call the right friend, get a coach, do whatever it takes. A negative attitude will never lead you to "the one." If you lose faith, stop dating for a while and do the hard work you need to do to shift your mindset back to where it needs to be. The stakes are just too damn high, and I want you to find your man. Remember the comic I shared with you. Do not let yourself get discouraged and give up. You are closer to love than you think. As long as you can maintain a positive attitude, make a consistent effort and use the strategies in this book, you will be successful.

FINDING HIM

I'm excited for you to find your person and to start the next chapter of your lives together. If you can navigate the obstacles, stick to the plan, and get support when you need it, I know you'll find your guy.

There are going to be times when you want to give up. Don't. If you do, you'll end up exactly where you've been. In order to get a different outcome, you need to step outside of your comfort zone and do things differently. Get the support you need, make time for dating because it's your number one priority, lean into the discomfort, trust the process, let go of control, and have some faith.

Stop judging and making assumptions and letting your ego do the picking for you. Don't let the bright shiny object take you off track and waste your time. Let go of the drama and get comfortable with a nice guy. And if the journey gets hard, get centered, stay positive, reboot and keep going. You have too much to gain to let anything stop you. Finding the love of your life is worth it. You can do this. I believe in you.

13

YOU'VE GOT THIS

I'm quite a private person, and I'm not one to share my experiences with people I don't know. But because the lessons I learned on my journey to find my husband have helped so many of my clients find love, I thought I should share my stories and those same time-tested strategies with you here. I'm so glad you've journeyed through this book with me and have opened your mind to a new way of dating.

I know you're frustrated. And I know you're ready. Now that you have the information in this book, I hope you see the light at the end of the tunnel. I hope you appreciate how logical these five strategic steps are. I've shared them with you because, whatever your happily-ever-after looks like, I want you to have it. You deserve to have your dreams come true.

WHILE WINDOW SHOPPING

A few months ago, I was walking in town running errands
and window shopping when I noticed a young woman
sitting on a bench with a baby in her arms. Something
about her caught my eye, and as I passed her, I realized
who she was. It was my former client Claire. The last time
I'd heard from her, she was newly married to her husband
Tim who she'd met on Match.com while working with
me. Do you remember her from the story I told about the
two of them heading to a resort to share a special weekend? When Claire and I first met, she was in her late thirties and so tired of dating the wrong men. She hired me
because she desperately wanted to get married and have a
family. When I met Claire, she'd been dating on
Match.com for two straight years with no success, and
she'd just frozen her eggs.

As soon as I realized it was Claire on the bench, I
stopped and said hello. She looked up at me with a big
smile. Then Claire stood up and introduced me to the
beautiful baby boy in her arms. His eyes were bright blue.
I asked about Tim and her son, we chatted for a few
minutes and then said our goodbyes. As I turned to walk
away, she said, "Thank you so much, Michelle. I'm so glad
I decided to work with you. I got everything I wanted."
She looked down at her infant son and then at me again.
"He's beautiful," I said. "I'm so happy for you." I walked
away with a huge smile on my face, and a full heart.
Moments like that are the reason I do what I do. They feel
like magic.

LOVE IS ALL THERE IS

I've spent a lot of time pondering the meaning of life, why we're all here on this planet making our way around the sun together. Here's what I've come up with. We're here to learn, to grow, and to master the art of love and compassion for ourselves and for each other, that's what I believe. Love is why we're here. And love is the reason I decided to become a matchmaker and a dating and relationship coach over a decade ago. It's also the reason, I enjoy my job every single day. When you strip everything else away, love is all there is. Relationships are what make our lives full. We love our families and our community of friends very much. But it's the love we give and receive from our partner that can be the most fulfilling. And yet love is so elusive. I often wonder why that is. Why is finding romantic love and getting it right such a challenge? I'm sure you've wondered the same thing. Why is it so hard for a kind, loving, deserving person like you to find your partner? After all you've been through and all you've tried, why haven't you met him yet? There's a bigger plan that you simply cannot see, and you have to have faith. If you do your part and implement your new approach and strategy, the Universe will take care of the rest.

Like you, I've loved several men over the years, and some of them have hurt me. Even so, I don't regret loving them one bit. Why? Because I learned so much from those relationships. The lessons I learned, while painful, have brought me to this moment and have made me who I am today. In addition, those experiences, and the insights I gained from them, have given me the ability to help hundreds of people find love and have better relation-ships. When I look back, I wouldn't change a thing. And while my exes aren't my favorite people by a long shot, I'm deeply grateful we crossed paths. I believe the people who have hurt us are our greatest teachers. And so, I'm grateful for the lessons that have made me who I am today.

IT'S MEANT TO BE

I hope you, too, are able to let go of any anger, pain or regret and can instead embrace the lessons you've received along the way knowing they were meant especially for you. Please don't beat yourself up for making the choices you made. You had certain needs that were being fulfilled at the time, and there were lessons you needed to receive. Because of those experiences, you've grown so much. I hope you'll reflect and ask yourself, "What have I learned?" And even ponder the bigger question, "What am I here to learn?" For many of my clients the answer has been, "I'm here to learn how to love myself enough to put myself first." That's hard for a lot of women to do. That's okay. We're all works in progress. Please be kind to yourself and always look for the lessons.

I believe we have multiple soulmates who touch our lives for many reasons. Some souls come and go, and others stay with us throughout our lives. I try to cultivate gratitude for the love and lessons each of my soulmates has brought to my life, even if they were just passing through for a little while. I hope you'll do the same. Every soul is on its own journey. As we receive life's lessons and say goodbye to the soulmates who aren't meant to stay, let's forgive them. Let's send them love and wish them well as we move on with our lives.

When you look in the mirror, I hope you love and admire the woman you see. Not just the symmetry, the curves and lines of your face, but the soul inside your eyes, the culmination of your years, and the fullness of your beautiful heart. I hope you're proud of all you've accomplished, even if your story is imperfect, it's uniquely yours. Embrace it. Appreciate who you've become. You're amazing. You're so strong. You're absolutely spectacular.

PUTTING IT ALL TOGETHER

My most sincere wish is that the lessons and stories in this book are helpful to you. Sometimes, making even a small change to the way you approach something can make a significant difference. But when you make big changes, like the ones I've asked you to make in this book, like leaning in and changing your mindset, viewing others with an open mind and an open heart, and incorporating my five-step strategy to date in a whole new way, it will literally change your life.

I've got the most wonderful news for you. When you do things differently, you'll get a completely different result. The decisions you make create the life you live. You have the power to create the future you want. I've given you the tools and taught you how to push the men who waste your time out of the way so you can move down the "football field" toward your husband. You've written a protective contract and have strong boundaries in place so you will never waste time on a man who treats you poorly again. You've also written your list of needs so you know exactly what your dealbreakers are, what you must have to feel treasured, fulfilled and safe in your future relationship. You've carefully considered your preferences and know what you want but won't let that long list stand in the way of getting what you need. You understand that preferences are just that, they're preferences. Moving forward, you're going to focus on the things that matter, the things that will impact your happiness and make a man a wonderful partner to you.

My hope is that, as you read this book, you've recognized your blind spots. Now that you know what they are, I hope you'll navigate dating differently with a new, smarter strategy. I also hope you're ready to make your search for love your number one priority. You'll need to make time for dating and for your new relationship. If you need to make some changes to your life so that's possible, please do. It will be worth it. I assure you, when you focus your time and effort on getting exactly what you want, the Universe will deliver.

I've taught you where to find quality men and also shared how to meet them. Now that you know they're literally everywhere, both online and around you every single day, I hope you'll engage more often, smile more frequently and even talk to strangers. They won't bite! I hope you'll use the lessons in this book to connect with men more authentically and more compassionately. Remember, some good guys are bad at dating, so cut them some slack. Look for the gooey center in every single person you meet. Make new friends. Have more fun every single day. Think outside of your box.

I hope I've left you with a deeper understanding of how men think and date so you can navigate with confidence. Playing poker, and putting the onus on men to create momentum, will attract a giver who's genuinely excited about you. It will also keep you in your feminine energy, which is your superpower and will attract the kind of man you want to meet. And even though you'll be tempted, I hope you understand why waiting to have sex until you're in a relationship is so important. When you wait, men who aren't that into you or who can't commit will disappear. Don't be upset if that happens. Instead, be grateful he exited early and didn't waste any more of your valuable time. A man who understands how amazing you are and sees you as his potential partner will have no problem waiting. He'll respect your boundaries because he wants to make you feel comfortable and knows you're worth the wait.

THE FASTEST WAY TO FIND HIM

You deserve to have an amazing partner, so don't let anything stand in the way. One of my favorite things to say is, "The fastest way to find the right man is to get rid of the wrong man quickly." This is true without a doubt. Now that you know exactly what your needs are, and you have strong boundaries in place. I hope you will quickly identify red flags and then advocate for yourself right away. I've demonstrated how important it is to walk away from relationships that aren't serving you, and I've given you specific language to use when red flags appear. I've shown you how to determine when to stay or when it's time to move on. I've even shared the kindest way to say goodbye to someone who isn't the right fit for you. I hope you'll always be decisive but also be kind. When you walk away from the wrong man, you will make space in your life for the right man. I hope you will date from a place of abundance instead of from scarcity. I hope you'll have faith that the Universe will deliver your husband. I assure you, it will.

THE EQUATION

Remember this equation:

The right mindset + the right strategy + consistent effort = your husband!

Stay positive, take off your dating goggles, use the tools in this book, and consistently make an effort. If you do those things, you cannot fail.

FORGETTING CHRISTMAS

I'm going to leave you with one last story – one that makes me smile every time I think about it. Recently, I was on a coaching call with my client Alexa who confided that none of her former boyfriends had ever remembered her birthday. Can you imagine that? Not a single one remembered her special day. That must have felt terrible. I was working from home that day, and my husband was nearby, so I called him over and asked him to join us on our video call. I explained to Rob that none of Alexa's boyfriends had ever remembered her birthday, and I asked him what he thought about that. Do you know what Rob said? "Those guys were complete assholes who didn't deserve you. If I forgot Michelle's birthday, it would be like forgetting Christmas," he said. And this from a man who is obsessed with Christmas. God, I love the way he loves me. His words were exactly what Alexa needed to hear. I'm happy to report that she is currently dating the most wonderful and thoughtful man who absolutely adores her. And guess what? He remembered her birthday.

So here are my parting words to you. Date a man who thinks your birthday is as important as Christmas (or whatever holiday he loves the most). Find a man who adores you, who wakes up every day knowing how lucky he is to be with you, and who shows you he feels that way every single day. Find a man who will stand by you through everything, no matter what comes up in life, the good and the bad. Find a man who's willing to be in the garden with you, who will weed with you every single day, who will show up and do the work, so your relationships can blossom and grow.

Most importantly – and pardon my French – don't fucking settle for a man who doesn't deserve you ever again. I'll leave it at that. Now, go on and find "the one." He's out there looking for you right now.

ABOUT THE AUTHOR

Michelle Jacoby is a matchmaker, dating and relationship coach, and the owner of DC Matchmaking, a small boutique matchmaking and coaching company for commitment-minded singles in the Washington, DC, area. She is also the co-founder of The Matchmakers Alliance, an organization that brings together top matchmakers and coaches from all over the world to collaborate and learn from one another. Michelle teaches body language for dating and runs Smart Dating Boot Camps™ for single women.

Michelle was voted Best Matchmaker in the US at the 2017 iDate Awards. She was awarded finalist for Best Matchmaker and/or Best Dating Coach in the industry at the 2015 iDate Awards, the 2016 US Dating Awards, and the 2018 and 2020 iDate Awards. Michelle has been a featured speaker for many years at national matchmaking conferences and at iDate, the dating industry's largest conference. She also participated in The Great Love Debate. Michelle has appeared in *The Washington Post*, *The Northwest and Georgetown Currents*, *The Washington Examiner*, *Bethesda Magazine*, WUSA Channel 9, News Channel 8's *Let's Talk Live*, WJLA's *Good Morning Washington*, NBC Washington, *Huffington Post*, ABC, FOX, NPR, and Newsy. Her articles have been featured in *Self*, *Washington Life Magazine*, *Fairfax Woman Magazine*, *Southern Woman Magazine*, YourTango.com, ThoughtCatalog.com, eharmony Advice, and Yahoo.

With a loving hand and an authentic voice, Michelle offers clear actionable advice so singles are empowered to finally find healthy, happy, and sustainable relationships.

Michelle lives in the Washington, DC, Area with her husband and has four children.

www.DCMatchmaking.com
www.MichelleJacoby.com
Michelle@MichelleJacoby.com
Instagram: @Michelle_Jacoby
Twitter: @MJLoveCoach
Facebook: www.facebook.com/MJLoveCoach
Clubhouse: @MichelleJacoby

ABOUT DIFFERENCE PRESS

Difference Press is the exclusive publishing arm of The Author Incubator, an educational company for entrepreneurs – including life coaches, healers, consultants, and community leaders – looking for a comprehensive solution to get their books written, published, and promoted. Its founder, Dr. Angela Lauria, has been bringing to life the literary ventures of hundreds of authors-in-transformation since 1994.

A boutique-style self-publishing service for clients of The Author Incubator, Difference Press boasts a fair and easy-to-understand profit structure, low-priced author copies, and author-friendly contract terms. Most importantly, all of our #incubatedauthors maintain ownership of their copyright at all times.

LET'S START A MOVEMENT WITH YOUR MESSAGE

In a market where hundreds of thousands of books are published every year and are never heard from again, The Author Incubator is different. Not only do all Difference Press books reach Amazon bestseller status, but all of our authors are actively changing lives and making a difference.

Since launching in 2013, we've served over 500 authors who came to us with an idea for a book and were able to write it and get it self-published in less than six months. In addition, more than 100 of those books were picked up by traditional publishers and are now available in bookstores. We do this by selecting the highest quality and highest potential applicants for our future programs.

Our program doesn't only teach you how to write a book – our team of coaches, developmental editors, copy editors, art directors, and marketing experts incubate you from having a book idea to being a published, best-selling author, ensuring that the book you create can actually make a difference in the world. Then we give you the training you need to use your book to make the difference in the world, or to create a business out of serving your readers.

ARE YOU READY TO MAKE A DIFFERENCE?

You've seen other people make a difference with a book. Now it's your turn. If you are ready to stop watching and start taking massive action, go to http://theauthorincubator.com/apply/.

"Yes, I'm ready!"

OTHER BOOKS BY DIFFERENCE PRESS

The Well-Paid Christian: A Spirit-Centered Guide to Showing up as Your Best Self in Society by Lauren Ahmadian

Relentless to Rise: Powering Your Life from the Inside-Out by Kathleen Black

Happy Teachers, Joyful Students, Engaged Families: A Guide for Building a School Community That Works by Donna Marie Cozine, Ed.D.

Teach and Stay Sane: A Teacher's Guide to Streamlining Work and Life by Danielle E. Felton

Life with a Service Dog: Make an Informed Decision to Get a Psychiatric Service Dog by Chelsea Liebowitz

The Confident Parent: A Recipe of Hope for Struggling Kids & Striving Parents by Melissa Lopez-Larson, M.D.

Stop Sabotaging Your Weight Loss: Why You Do It and How to Fix It by Jennifer Powter, MSc

Is Coaching Your Calling?: How to Be Successful as a Transformational Coach by Kelley Oswin, RSW, Ernie Pavan, and Laura Slinn

Intuitive and Psychic Development: A Beginner's Guide to Deepening Your Spiritual Gifts by Kim Weaver

My Covid-19 Diary: Practical Tips and Scriptures for Improbable Times from an American Doctor by Theresa Y. Wee, M.D.

THANK YOU

Thank you so much for reading my book! Now that you've learned a completely new approach to dating, I hope you're feeling super empowered and excited to go find "the one"!

As a thank you and to help you take action right away, I'm happy to schedule a call with you so we can connect personally, and I can help you to come up with a plan.

Email me at mj@DCMatchmaking.com, and I'll respond quickly. I'm excited to hear from you!

xo,
Michelle

Printed in Great Britain
by Amazon

20644642R00120